"In this beautiful book, Bill Damon simultaneously reviews his life and that of the father he never met. Two lives in review, two stories, two journeys that hold lessons for all of us about how to forgive ourselves and others, how to appreciate ourselves and others, and by making peace with the past find our way forward."

—**Angela Duckworth**, PhD, founder and CEO of Character Lab and author of *Grit*

"From one of America's foremost scholars of purpose in life comes a blueprint for a more fulfilling, grateful, and joyous life."

—**Marc Freedman**, CEO, Encore.org, and author of *How to Live Forever*

"This extraordinary memoir depicts the powerful insights that can emerge from reflecting on one's personal history and life work."

—**Howard Gardner**, PhD, Hobbs Research Professor of Cognition and Education, Harvard Graduate School of Education, and author of *A Synthesizing Mind*

"[Damon's] autobiographical account is original, candid, and poignant, full of irony and humor. This splendid, rich volume tells the story of coming to terms with one's past to face the present, and demonstrates the redemptive, reinvigorating power of looking back on one's life."

—**Vartan Gregorian**, president of Carnegie Corporation of New York

"More than just an intriguing and fascinating memoir written in an engagingly narrative style, Damon enables readers to appreciate deeply the universal significance of family relationships for finding meaning, value, identity, and purpose in life. Damon's work is a unique guide for all readers to review and embrace their own life journey."

—**Richard M. Lerner**, Bergstrom Chair in Applied Developmental Science, and director, Institute for Applied Research in Youth Development, Tufts University

"The book blends personal experience and psychological theory to consider the mysteries of memory and identity in human lives and the power of self-acceptance, forgiveness, and gratitude. If, as Aristotle wrote, living life well is like playing a musical instrument with skill and beauty, William Damon proves to be a virtuoso."

—**Dan P. McAdams**, the Henry Wade Rogers Professor of Psychology, Northwestern University

"William Damon's *A Round of Golf with My Father* defies categorization. It is a gripping detective story, a deeply touching personal memoir, a critique of developmental psychology, a compendium of life-giving maxims, and a celebration of disciplined life review. Once I started reading it, I had a hard time putting it down."

—**Michael Murphy**, cofounder of the Esalen Institute and author of *Golf in the Kingdom* and *The Future of the Body*

"Part detective story, part thriller, and part psychological masterclass, Bill Damon's *A Round of Golf with My Father* is a must-read. By taking us on a deeply personal journey into his own past, this inspiring and remarkable book could not arrive at a better time."

—**Henry Timms**, coauthor of the bestseller *New Power*, cofounder of #GivingTuesday, and president of Lincoln Center

Also by William Damon

The Power of Ideals (with Anne Colby)
The Path to Purpose
The Moral Advantage
Noble Purpose
Good Work (with Howard Gardner and Mihaly Csikszentmihalyi)
The Youth Charter
Greater Expectations
Some Do Care (with Anne Colby)
The Moral Child
Self-Understanding in Childhood and Adolescence (with Daniel Hart)
Social and Personality Development
The Social World of the Child

A Round *of* Golf
with My Father

A Round *of* Golf *with* My Father

*The New Psychology of Exploring Your Past
to Make Peace with Your Present*

William Damon

TEMPLETON PRESS

TEMPLETON PRESS
300 Conshohocken State Road, Suite 500
West Conshohocken, PA 19428
www.templetonpress.org

This paper meets the requirements of ANSI/NISO Z39.48-1992
(Permanence of Paper).

ISBN: 978-1-59947-596-7 (paper)
ISBN: 978-1-59947-564-6 (ebook)

Library of Congress Control Number: 2021932150

A catalogue record for this book is available from the Library of Congress.

Printed in the United States of America.

22 23 24 25 26   10 9 8 7 6 5 4 3 2 1

To Jesse, Maria, Caroline, Sarah, and Isak

CONTENTS

PROLOGUE

A Call of Consequence

"DAD, I DON'T know if I should be telling you about this."

The call came from my daughter Maria one afternoon while I was sitting in my office in California. There was uncharacteristic hesitation in her voice.

A spirited, world-traveling young economist, Maria was in Cape Town, South Africa, on a teaching assignment. Jet lag had kept her up late that night. She'd used her sleepless time to dig into some "family stuff" online—stuff that might interest me or might upset me, she didn't know which. But her findings were so fascinating she really wanted to share them with me. Finally, she decided that I probably could handle it.

In that consequential call, my daughter introduced me to my father.

During her sleepless night in Cape Town, Maria had become curious about a grandfather she never knew. That man was also the father I never knew. Oddly, I had never shared Maria's curiosity, a lack of interest that I'd never questioned before but which now seemed mysterious to me. As it turned out, Maria's call uncovered many mysteries that had long been buried in the conspiracy of family silence that had surrounded me as a child. I listened intently as she opened the doors to the long-locked vault of my family history.

She was right: I did handle it without getting upset. In fact, Maria's online discoveries intrigued and thrilled me in a way that took both of us by surprise. What she revealed set me off on my own ten-year discovery quest. It led me to a new understanding of myself and the course my life had taken. It triggered a process of reflection that helped me gain perspective on the choices I've made and helped me think more clearly about the choices in front of me.

The introduction to my father did not take place in person, nor could it. By the time Maria "found" him, he had been dead for twenty years. I didn't know this, or much of anything else about him at that time. But as a result of Maria's call, I was introduced to my father as a person—a person with physical features I could gaze at in old black-and-white photos, a life story I could investigate, living friends and relatives whom I could meet, and character traits I could uncover, analyze, and compare with my own.

I had lived for more than six decades without seeing a picture of him. As a fatherless boy, I had found father figures to guide me through the uncertain and aspirational phases of growing up. Yet the man himself had been entirely missing from my life. Now, after all these years, I was offered a glimpse of the actual man. What was he like? What happened to him? What did he do with his life?

Until college, all I knew about my father was that he was "missing in World War II." I assumed he had died in action on some nameless European battlefield. Then, in the midst of my college years, I heard otherwise, in cryptic information that my mother revealed to me in a brief remark. But at that time I had no interest in following up on anything I may have heard about my missing father. I was absorbed in my studies, and then in my career, and then in my own growing family. I was not at all eager to get distracted by emotionally loaded information concerning a man who apparently had abandoned my mother and me as soon as I was born.

As a result, I knew virtually nothing about what became of my father after he had left the one mark on the world that *was* obvious to me: the act of inseminating my mother. The context of that act, all-important as it was for me and my children, remained as cloaked in mystery as the rest of my father's story.

When I answered Maria's call, little did I know that it was to take me on a journey that would make a trip from California to Cape Town feel like walking down the block. It turned out to be a journey that brought me back to my childhood years, and then back even deeper into the twentieth century and some of its great dramas. My father's disappearance, in addition to its profound effect on my life, was bound up in historic stories of World War II, the Cold War, the 1960s civil rights movement, and the postwar American diplomatic mission of promoting democracy throughout the world. Like all lives, my own has been shaped by the historic periods I've lived through. Now I had a further insight to consider: the way my father's life reflected the era he lived through and to which, in small but significant ways, he contributed.

All this shook my sense of my own life's trajectory to its foundations. I felt drawn into a reconsideration of where I came from, how I got to where I am now, and why I made the choices that have made me the person I am. I had an intimation that such reconsideration might guide me in directions yet to come. By gaining an understanding of my roots, I gained a clearer hold on my future. By filling in long-standing elements of my identity that had been concealed from me, I was offered a new chance to develop in ways that would advance purposes I have long held dear.

I could do none of this without some method of self-examination. I was embarking on a serious quest, and I knew that I would not get very far if I approached it casually or haphazardly. Part of the quest—the reconstruction of my father's life—was historical, which required digging through old archives and interviewing his still-living friends and relatives. I am not a historian by training, so my efforts on this were dedicated but amateurish. The other part of the quest, which I saw as essential, was psychological: using what I found to construct a transformed view of my own life, one that could provide me with renewed purpose and direction. In this endeavor, I was able to draw on my professional knowledge as a life-span developmental psychologist who has explored purpose and identity in his research and writings.

But my own previous work in psychology was not in itself sufficient for the quest I was now embarking on. For the self-examination I was undertaking, I found a promising approach that has been emerging in clinical and autobiographical studies over the past two decades, called "the life review." A life review is a deliberate procedure for reconstructing our pasts in a manner that can provide three personal benefits that many of us desire as we grow older:

1. acceptance of the events and choices that have shaped our lives, reflecting gratitude for the life we've been given rather than self-doubt and regret

2. a more authentic (and thus more robust) understanding of who we are and how we got to be that way, reflecting the well-grounded, reassuring sense of self that the great psychologist Erik Erikson called "ego integrity"

3. a clarity in the directions we wish to take our lives going forward, reflecting what we have learned from the experiences and purposes that have given our lives meaning in the past

I adapted the general life review approach to my own particular circumstances and needs. I do not claim to have implemented or replicated the method in a rigorous and systematic way with a scientifically drawn sample of subjects. In fact, in my exploration there was only one subject: me. The life review approach gave me a way to investigate and construct the renovated life story that I needed to work out for myself. As I went about this, I increasingly came to believe that the approach could be helpful for others seeking renewed understandings of themselves and the way their lives and life purposes have evolved.

In discovering the truth about the man who sired me, I understood what I had missed in a childhood without a father. I came to terms with long-unacknowledged—or buried—resentments that I may have had as an only child growing up with a single mother. I acquired a sense of what I gained by learning to compensate for my father's absence. As strange as it may sound, I even learned what I owed him.

In the process, I've come to a new understanding of my struggles, my accomplishments, my mistakes, and most importantly the trail of purposes that have defined my highest aspirations and most gratifying contributions to the world. My life story, although not yet complete, is more filled in and more authentic. As such, I believe it offers me a truer guide going forward, one that is sturdier in its capacity to direct and sustain my future choices.

This book is about three journeys of discovery that have captured my imagination since my daughter's consequential call. The first is central to my professional work: a scientific quest to learn more about how people find purposeful identities that fulfill their lives. While my earlier research focused on younger people, in recent years I've turned to later periods of life, seeking to understand what purpose means for people who have much to look back on. The second journey is more personal, though it is widely shared: a desire to understand my past, present, and future in ways that provide reasons for satisfaction rather than regret or despair. By sharing reflections from my life review, I hope to inform readers about how life reviews offer opportunities to find renewed purpose and clarity of direction. The third journey is unique to me, and it sprang upon me unexpectedly: a historical quest to learn the truth about my missing father, through archival searches, interviews with his still-living friends and family, and travel to sites where he grew up, worked, and played. My goal here was to construct a portrait of my father's life that would not only satisfy my newly aroused curiosity but also inform my other two quests. I share the fruits of this unique historical quest to convey the intriguing facts that I discovered about my own life story and my father's, and also to share the special window they provide on key events in world history. Some of what I learned had moving personal meaning for me; and some of it qualifies as more general psychological and historical discovery.

The explorations in this book take place in a zone where psychological science, personal experience, and philosophical reflection meet. This is not the first time I've ventured into such territory. When I began the research that led to *The Path to Purpose*, the best-known treatments of purpose were found in philosophical and theological contemplations (such as Rick Warren's *The Purpose-Driven Life*) or self-help books (such as Richard Leider's *Power of Purpose*). By now, it's fair to say, purpose has become a well-established subject of study and practice in fields such as education, business, medicine, and psychology. I believe that the feelings that prompted me to write the present book are ones people everywhere will recognize: a quest to better understand my past and present self, my sense of loss for a key family member who went missing from my life, my confusion over long-ago childhood mysteries, my need to heal past wounds and regrets, and my wish to reaffirm the life I've been given.

Everyone searches for life meaning in a unique and personal way. But the search itself is universal. For those who choose to join me on the journeys contained in these pages, I hope that my research, my reflections, and my discoveries provide useful insights about this most personal, and most universal, human quest.

A Round *of* Golf
with My Father

1

Uncovering the Past

THE INFORMATION THAT my daughter Maria revealed to me in her consequential call had been surprisingly available for her to track down in our digital age. She knew that my father's (her grandfather's) name was Philip. She also knew a bit of family lore suggesting he may have been in Thailand for some reason. (When reminded, I recalled this trace of information too, although I did not remember how I came to know it or what it meant.) Maria googled "Philip Damon Thailand." Immediately the key that opened a long-shut vault appeared. It was an interview with a veteran diplomat named Kenneth MacCormac from an oral history that the now-closed USIA (United States Information Agency) commissioned after it began to wind down its operations in the late 1980s.

As soon as we ended our call, Maria emailed me the link to the interview. I downloaded it quickly and devoured it. In it, MacCormac discusses his many assignments around the world and speaks warmly about the colleagues who worked with him. His reminiscences shine with magnanimity and devotion to his country. His service was broad and deep, taking him to trouble spots around the world during decades of global conflict. He was a model of patriotism during what is now referred to as the "American Century." He was part of the "Greatest Generation" that Tom Brokaw eulogized in his book of that name.

In the middle of MacCormac's interview, without explanation, he was asked, "When you were in Thailand, did you know Phil Damon?" This very question added its own intrigue. Of all the diplomats, cultural attachés, and other State Department staff who were stationed in Thailand during MacCormac's years there, why was Phil Damon (*my father*, as I now began calling him in my mind) singled out in this way? What was my father doing over there anyway?

The intrigue of the question paled before the gleaming nuggets of new information buried in MacCormac's answers. I stared at the following sentences as if they were a treasure chest that I stumbled upon during a chance stroll on a long-deserted beach:

MacCormac: Yes. Philip Damon, whom I'd known in my German days in Germany, and who had married a delightful French girl who came with the ballet from Nice to Munich, he was in Bangkok when I got there. Phil and Genevieve Damon were very close to the king and queen. They were both fluent in French, and Phil was a big, outgoing guy, a great golfer, but sadly enough, he contracted multiple sclerosis, and he was back in Washington when this developed. He always thought if he could get back to Thailand, he'd get better, but, of course, he didn't. Through agency help, he was brought back to Thailand as an employee without compensation, I think it was called. There he had the use of the APO and the commissary. The king and queen kept him in Chulalongkorn hospital with day and night nurses for the first year he was there. Phil is still living. I go to see him whenever I go to Bangkok. He's totally bedridden. I think he's nearly blind. His only source of happiness is the books on records which he gets from the Library of Congress.

Questioner: Is his association with the king terminated now?

MacCormac: No. The associations with the king and queen are still strong. As a matter of fact, his wife, Genevieve, is a great friend of the queen's, and Genevieve is the only non-Thai that I know of who has been given a title by the king. She's now known as Khun Ying Damon. She runs a small ballet school, and she's been a marvelous, marvelous wife to Philip Damon, who has had this terrible affliction. His three daughters are now married and living in Thailand.

Well . . . this was a lot to "process," as they say in the psychological counseling industry. I couldn't take it all in. The main thing that struck me at first was the least exotic item on the list. *He was a "great golfer"!* This thought, among all the other revelations, was the one that bowled me over. I ran this over and over in my mind, ignoring for the moment all the rest of the amazing information disclosed in the interview.

Why did I ignore all the rest in that moment? That was the first question I asked myself in my emerging life review. It was a productive question, because it uncovered troubling feelings that I had never allowed myself to admit or remedy. The question helped me realize that, despite my lifelong nonchalance regarding my father's absence and my apparent indifference to his fate, I actually did have a deep-seated emotional stake in who he was and what happened to him in his life without me.

Despite my seeming lack of interest over my entire previous life, as soon as I got a taste of real information about my father, I found it so highly charged that my initial reaction was to bat away most of it until I regained my equilibrium. The fragment that I didn't shut down was MacCormac's "great golfer" comment. This offhand remark opened a window onto a central element in my unexplored cache of buried feelings: a resentment that I had never allowed myself to recognize. It was when I encountered the words "great golfer" next to my father's name that I first consciously felt this resentment. It was an unexpected reaction, unpleasant and unwanted. No wonder I had always tried to avoid feeling that way! Later, as I went further into my life review, this sup-pressed resentment emerged slowly but inexorably across a broader span of unfulfilled fatherly services.

Why, I grumbled to myself when I first read MacCormac's words, *couldn't my father at least have taught me golf?* I've loved golf ever since I found an inexpensive muni course near my home when I was in middle school. I worked hard to improve my game but was only self-taught. I never had lessons as a child. I never had anyone to show me the right techniques. Unlike my missing father, I never came anywhere near to being a "great golfer."

When I began my family discovery quest, my golf resentment stood glaringly alone for a long time. It was the one grievance I would acknowledge. My initial unawareness of any other grievances now seems strange to me, and it also seemed strange to others, especially previously unknown relatives I would meet for the first time. They would turn to the one certain fact we knew about my father: he did not return home to me after the war. He never visited, he never wrote, and he never saw to it that I knew anything about him. When I'd meet a mem-ber of my newly discovered family, the question arose, "Why aren't you bitter?"

It was true that I never appeared, to myself or anyone else, to be angry with my father for abandoning me. I thought hard about why this was so, but I would come up blank, other than some generalized senti-ments of gratitude, such as "I've had a good run in life. I wouldn't be here without my father, so what's there to complain about?" There is much truth to these sentiments, as platitudinous as they sound. But at most they were only part of my emotional picture. Figuring out the rest was a central task for my life review. It was one that would take some time.

Eventually, reading over the MacCormac interview again, my golf grievance dissipated in waves of fascination that swept over me as I read his description of my "big, outgoing" father married to a "delightful"

French ballerina. The trappings of royalty (kings, queens, royal titles) added a bit of sparkle to the picture, but what mesmerized me was the suddenly disclosed image of my father with a career in the Foreign Service and a full family life. To the extent I ever had thought about him at all, I had imagined him, in my immature mind, as a no-account loser who ran away from all his responsibilities, drifting off into oblivion like some pitiable wayward detritus. I clearly had been very mistaken. He obviously had done lots of serious and productive things in his life. I was moved by the sad image of him dying of an incurable disease. There was information here that would keep my head spinning for years to come. I would find some of the revelations heartening and others imbued with loss and regret.

I am a developmental psychologist. I've dedicated my career to exploring how people make pivotal life choices, find purposes that drive them, and construct identities that enable them to become the kinds of people they wish to be. Now I had my father's life to explore with this professional lens—and my own life to reexamine in the process. Despite my father's permanent absence, my life had been inextricably bound up with his in ways that I was only just beginning to grasp.

After digesting the initial revelations in the MacCormac interview, I began a five-year discovery search for archival records that would shed light on my father's school, military, and Foreign Service engagements. I searched for online digital records, and I searched in file cabinets for paper records that had never been digitized. One moment I was googling leads on my iPhone, and the next moment I was rifling through crumbling documents and faded photos in worn paper folders. I visited libraries, archives, the British War Museum in London, and Pittsfield, Massachusetts, the small city where my father grew up, searching everywhere for documents that noted him. I was amazed at how thrilling it is to find firsthand historical information in old documents. It felt like detective work. I now understood why ancestry searches have become one of the burgeoning avocations of our era.

Two Ways That Our Pasts Hold
Secrets from Us

Everyone's past is full of secrets. This is not to say that we intentionally keep our pasts hidden (although there may be times when we don't wish to disclose certain events to others). Most frequently, our pasts hold secrets that keep earlier events hidden *from ourselves*. We may not be aware that the secrets exist in the first place; or if we are aware of them, we may not be able to comprehend them through the powers of intellect available to us.

A life review can be a means for uncovering parts of our past that remain hidden from us. And, as in my case, a life review might be triggered by the uncovering of an old secret that has concealed parts of our pasts that are important for us to understand, an understanding now made possible by the new revelation.

Two types of secrets keep important parts of our pasts hidden from us. The first type is a lack of full knowledge about all the people and events that have played a role in our lives. This is to some extent inevitable: we simply can't know everything that happened with our ancestors, or even with our immediate families. Some facts may have been deliberately hidden from us or never mentioned. Wartime hardships and economic reversals might be avoided in family conversations because they are too painful to discuss. A family member who went astray and violated the family's code of values might be left out of conversations. You might wonder, *Why does no one ever talk about what happened to Uncle Ted?* But this might not be a question you can ask out loud as a child. Or you might never learn that he existed. The memory of a firstborn who died as an infant could be too painful for grieving parents to mention, so their later children grow up never knowing they had a sibling—perhaps until their aging mother, slipping into dementia, begins whispering an unfamiliar child's name. Wild and crazy adventures of a grandparent might be overshadowed by decades of domestic life, all but forgotten until a cache of newspaper clippings discovered in the attic tells a whole different story about the old person you always thought was so conventional. Suicide, alcoholism, or criminality in a family might be concealed out of shame. Lifestyles that were once unacceptable might have been covered up or denied. The "maiden aunt" who lived with her female companion would be described very differently in today's culture than she had been in her own time.

In the course of a life review, as we learn more about our family's history and our own, we may come upon information that informs or surprises us, causing us to think differently about people or events. We may rewrite earlier stories and question our long-held assumptions. We may feel that we now are getting to know our loved ones, and ourselves, all over again.

The second type of secret is internal to us. Our memories are far from perfect records of what actually happened in our pasts. Memories are to a large extent constructions that reflect a combination of our present feelings, our biases, things we have learned to believe, and recalled traces of the actual events. As such, our memories often are flawed by omissions, distortions, and unconsciously invented details. For this reason, our memories themselves often contain secrets that keep the whole story of our actual pasts hidden from us. This is particularly common in the case of traumatic events. Survivors of natural catastrophes may retain no clear memories of their experiences. Memories that make us uncomfortable also may be suppressed. Embarrassing faux pas may be written out of our minds because thinking of them would make us quiver with shame.

In my efforts to reconstruct my own past for my life review, both types of secrets—a lack of information and memory imperfections—were staunchly in place. While I was growing up in my mother's home, she and the other adults in my life encased me in a bubble of ignorance about my father that was impossible for a child to penetrate. Whenever the subject of my father's whereabouts came up, my mother would say no more than that he was "missing in World War II." This curt response swiftly closed off further dialogue, both within the family and outside it. That phrase became my reply to the outside world, a rote response requiring no further comment on my part. And it was not just that phrase I adopted; I also took on an overriding lack of interest in anything that had to do with the man who had fathered me.

As I grew past childhood, clues started appearing that I now vaguely recall, although at the time I ignored or misunderstood them. When I was a sophomore in college, my mother offhandedly mentioned that she had been in touch with my father, asking if I would like a share of the small monthly child support funds she was then receiving. This was the first I ever heard that my father was, in fact, still alive. But at that time, with a fully engaged college life, I had no interest in finding out any more about this man who I now figured was a deadbeat who had abandoned his family and disappeared in some nether regions of life. That conversation with my mother was awkward and never resumed.

Consequently, before my life review, I was blithely heedless of the facts surrounding my father. I needed to uncover those facts in order to find out all the ways in which this man I never knew had influenced my life. What's more, when I retrieved those facts, I became aware of how flawed my memories were regarding possible clues about my father that may have arisen in my earlier years.

In order to address both kinds of secrets, my life review needed both a family-historical discovery search and a mindful memory-reconstruction effort. The first informed the second. The information I uncovered stirred up recollections long lost to my mind. Some of the recollections endured only as distant and confused memory traces, so far out of reach that I was never able to fully grasp them. The way I had buried them in my mind told me something I needed to know about my real feelings toward my missing father. The submerged feelings, wrapped up in my eroded, lost, or distorted memories, were a part of the life story I was trying to understand and clarify.

The life story that I was able to piece together through these efforts may seem unusual to those who read it. It has a long-missing parent, personal struggles, historical dramas, international intrigues, and many other colorful details. Yet everyone's story is, in its own way, unique, sometimes mysterious, often colorful, and always interesting. Everyone has moments of personal struggle. Everyone is a part of history and partakes in the historical dramas of the times. Everyone's past has a mystery (or two, or three, or more) that might be useful to clear up. Also, as I have found, many people have a family member who has gone missing at some point.

Naturally, to me, my own story, wrapped up with that of my missing father, seemed vivid and intriguing. I was enthralled by the idea of exploring it through a life review. I had the sense, from reading Robert Butler, Erik Erikson, Dan McAdams, and others who have written about identity formation and renewal, that an improved understanding of my past could point the way to present and future psychological benefits such as affirmation, gratitude, and diminished regrets. I offer my explorations here with the hope that readers too will find them interesting and informative, in part because they demonstrate potential fruits of intentional explorations of the past. I think that others who embark on similar journeys to explore hidden parts of their pasts could find their own stories at least as fascinating and informative.

Connecting Long-Lost Family Ties

Once I digested the information disclosed by Maria's call, and energized by the thrill of that discovery, I searched my memory for anything that might help advance the life review that I now determined to conduct. I recalled that as a child I had briefly and sporadically known my father's mother, "Grandmother Damon," as I was told to call her. She never visited me, but occasionally she invited me to the large Boston apartment that she shared with four elderly ladies who were introduced to me as "the aunts." I visited Grandmother Damon in this way perhaps four or five times in my elementary school years. My father was never mentioned, nor were there any pictures of him in her apartment. I remember enjoying these visits because one of the ladies, my great-aunt Agnes, was an avid Red Sox fan. We'd talk about Ted Williams and his flowing swing. I don't remember what I spoke about with Grandmother Damon, but I do recall her as a warm and kindly person.

As I took myself back to those visits, I found that I retained at least one important detail: my grandmother had a daughter named Verna, my father's sister. She was my Aunt Verna. I had no memory of meeting Aunt Verna, but her name had stuck in my mind. A quick internet search revealed that my long-lost Aunt Verna was living quite openly in Princeton, New Jersey. Since Verna was younger than my father by seven years, she was alive and well in her early eighties at the time I found her.

It took me a day to work up the courage to give Aunt Verna a call. When I did, she was wonderfully welcoming. She said that she had seen me once when I was a very young child and had heard a bit about my life since then. I told her I was eager to meet with her and find out as much as I could about my father and the family that has long been concealed from me. Verna warmly agreed to this. As soon as I got off the phone, I planned a trip with my wife, Anne, to the East Coast, with Princeton and Verna's home our ultimate destination. That visit, a few weeks later, would yield a host of new wonders. Eventually it would lead to my meeting Verna's two sons (my "new" first cousins) who over the twelve years since have become my dear friends. On the discovery front, that visit with Verna turned up one stunning bit of information that was to have a revolutionary effect on my sense of personal identity: *my father attended the same school that I went to twenty-two years later.* I discuss the profound significance of this new information in chapter 4.

There was more stunning information to be found online. I googled "Genevieve Damon," the name of my father's second wife. It turned out she was a notable part of the Thai cultural scene due to the ballet school she founded. I came up with a newspaper story about her in an online edition of a French-language newspaper, *Gavroche Thailand.* The story had this heading: "*Une ballerine franco-américaine à la Cour du Roi.*" I had learned a little French during a summer in Paris when I was a college student. There, in crisp, comprehensible French sentences, was a full account of Genevieve's career as a ballet performer, school founder, and instructor to the royal court in Thailand. My Parisian "stepmother" was a brilliant ballerina and grande dame.

The article also revealed that Genevieve had been a dedicated wife and mother. Passages described my father's life in Thailand with his family. I scanned the article to find an account of my father's years in Bangkok during the 1950s: "*Durant cette période, trois filles sont nées: Sumalie, Lawan et Pichitra, les deux dernières ayant reçu leur noms du Roi.*" He and Genevieve had three daughters, two of them named by the fabled king of Thailand.

Once again, this revelation parted the veils to a dim corner of my memory. The existence of my father's daughters was not exactly news to me, and as I deciphered the French words on the screen, a long-buried memory rose to the surface. Sometime in my mid-adult years, I had received a letter out of the blue from a young woman who introduced herself as my father's daughter. I vaguely remembered her name as "Patrisca," which was wrong: her actual name, I now found out, was Pichitra. She must have been about nineteen when she wrote her letter. At that time I was busily settling into my own home and family. I recall answering the letter with a polite postcard, thanking her for writing to me and noting that I had never had any contact with my father. I must have discarded Pichitra's first letter, because I no longer have it in my possession. Pichitra answered my brief postcard right away. I remembered that she wrote her second letter on the lightweight blue stationery that people once used for airmail, but I had no recollection of its contents, and I never thought of it again until that day, decades later, when I saw her name, along with those of her two sisters, in the French newspaper article. Suddenly I, raised as an only child, hungered to know my half sisters.

In the twenty-first century, how do you go about finding people when you have only names to go on? If the names are distinctive enough—and, fortunately, my sisters' names were unique—one solution is Facebook. It worked. I found profiles for two of the three sisters, Lawan and Sumali, and I sent them a message introducing myself and explaining who I was.

The first response came from Lawan. It was as friendly as I could have wished it to be:

> It was a very pleasant surprise for me, and I hope that I can get to know a bit about you and your family. I hope I am not being too forward, but you can't imagine how much curiosity my sister and I have about you! Yes, my [our] father was Philip, and [we had] a sister, Pichitra, who is no longer with us, having passed away almost 20 years ago, one year after our father.

This initial Facebook contact led to in-person visits that were sources of precious new information about my father and relationships with a delightful group of new family members—half sisters, nieces, and nephews. Everyone I met from Thailand was warm and welcoming, and I treasured all the "new" family members I discovered. I also deeply mourned the one I'd missed the chance to know.

The Sister I Never Met

A few months ago, after I began writing this book, I found Pichitra's second letter at the bottom of an old cardboard box in my garage. I was not looking for the letter, and I had no idea it would be there, buried underneath a pile of notebooks, pictures, and other memorabilia. With the timing of this accidental discovery, I almost believed the letter had been placed there by the hand of providence. When I saw Pichitra's letter again, I was stunned at how little I had remembered of its contents. I reread it now with fresh eyes, amazed that I did not pay more attention to it when I first received it.

Left to right, standing: Lawan Damon, Daniel Sundqvist, Kamolchat Anthony Piyavidyakarn, Luckhana Damon, Albert Damon, Sumali Damon; *seated:* Genevieve Lespagnol Damon, Maria Damon

"You probably know nothing about me," Pichitra wrote, "so I'll tell you what has happened to me by now." She went on to say that she had been born in Thailand, she lived there until she was four, and then she moved with the family to Washington when her father (and mine) was transferred back there. "I had quite a hard time at first because I couldn't speak English, but I soon learned it and, of course, forgot all my Thai." The letter went on to say that the family had returned to Thailand a few years later. "I had to learn Thai all over again, but this time I didn't forget English." She then finished high school at an international school in Bangkok and was enrolled as a first-year student in a college in Hawaii at the time of this letter. Reading those parts of Pichitra's letter after forty years, I am charmed by her brightness, warmth, and openness.

In that long-ago period when I received Pichitra's letter, my life was jammed with work and family responsibilities. My new career was a complicated mix of teaching, research, and writing. My young children were active, noisy, and curious and needed rides everywhere. I let Pichitra's second letter sit unattended for weeks on end, and those weeks turned into months. Eventually I stuck it somewhere out of sight without answering it. I don't know how the letter ended up at the bottom of that old cardboard box.

My jam-packed life from my thirties onward quickly erased any thoughts or recollections of Pichitra. Perhaps I was feeling averse toward my missing father, or perhaps my guilt over not answering the letter contributed to my amnesia. Whatever the reasons, Pichitra disappeared from my mind soon after I stowed her letter away and did not reappear until my daughter's phone call led me to contact her sisters over thirty years later.

Of the regrets in my life, failing to answer Pichitra's letter is at the very top, for many reasons. How I wish I could return to that time and write the affectionate response that was called for. She had reached out to me in an open and guileless way, with a wish to connect, and I didn't come through for her. It would have been a chance for me to enjoy relations with the Damon side of my family in midlife rather than decades later. And it would have given me a chance to meet my father in person while he was still alive (if I was ready to take that chance, which I can't honestly say I would have been). As I gaze at Pichitra's letter, I strongly sense that I would have liked (or loved) her as a sister, something that would have meant the world to me as an only child—and perhaps to her as well, as a girl with no brothers. Tragically, as I learned in Lawan's note, Pichitra died just a couple of years after writing that letter, forever removing my chance to know her.

One cruel thing about death is that it makes certain mistakes irreparable. With Pichitra now gone, I will never be able to meet her. With my father gone, I will never gain a full, flesh-and-blood sense of him.

With my mother gone, I will never be able to ask her the many questions that my recent discoveries have raised. These forsaken opportunities show how slowly I've come to understand the value of an extended family over the course of my life. This was something I needed to learn in adulthood, since I had so little experience with it when I was a child. I realize now how much fuller my life would have been if I had followed up on Pichitra's invitation to start making the connections that were there waiting for me. It's fortunate that we always have the capacity to learn, but I wish that we could learn important things more quickly. I'm reminded of a slogan I once saw written on the top of a beer mug that my great-uncle Louie kept on his desk: "We grow too soon old and too late smart."

A life review relies on explorations of the past and an openness to whatever lies hidden in its secrets. In my case, the secrets were made more obscure by my lack of interest in anything that had to do with my father, as well as my outright avoidance of any clues that popped up. For the early part of my life, my buried negative emotions fueled my spirit of avoidance. As a result, I learned little, and the few memories of anything I may have learned were rife with haziness and distortion.

At last, in my mid-sixties, I became open to learning about my father. I was at a point in life where I no longer felt threatened by whatever I might discover about him. Indeed, I felt a need to review my life story and pull together everything I could about how my life had been shaped, why it took the directions it did, and where it may be headed. I became eager to learn as much as I could about my father, his life history, and how his life shaped mine in ways that went beyond our biological link. The opportunity to uncover the secrets that had long obscured my father from me was made possible by the discovery of information that gave sense and substance to the uncertain memories I retained from my early days. My life review owes at least as much to this new information as to those shaky earlier memories.

Vagaries of Memory

A life review relies on reminiscences. Yet our memories (unlike, say, good photos) are unclear images clouded by our needs, desires, biases, and present states of mind. In interpreting reminiscences that make up the main part of a life review, it is important to recognize how our memories reflect not only what actually happened but also how we feel about what happened. In extreme instances, our memories reflect only what we mistakenly imagine to have happened.

Shortly after finishing graduate school, I received a small grant to visit the University of Geneva to sit in on a seminar given by one of my intellectual idols, legendary Swiss psychologist Jean Piaget. He was a grand old man with an imposing manner. Before I was introduced to him, I was told I shouldn't greet him with "*bonjour*" or "*ravi de vous rencontrer*," the normal French ways of saying "hello" or "pleased to meet you." Instead, I should utter "*honoré*," a deferential formalism meaning "honored to meet you." Piaget was known to staff and students as "*Le Patron*," implying that he was viewed as something between a boss and a father. One of his customs, which I've never dared imitate in my own teaching, was to dangle his pocket watch on a swinging chain in front of his class whenever a student spoke, stopping its swing only after the student finished. There were no long, rambling digressions in Piaget's seminar.

Piaget loved telling anecdotes and stories. He would become quite animated, and he had a famous twinkle in his eye whenever he talked of his childhood and youth. He told a story from his own life as a case in point when discussing the nature of memory. It was a dramatic tale of being grabbed by a kidnapper when he was lying in his baby carriage at around age three. He recounted this memory with great flourish, describing the black cape the kidnapper wore, the stalwart red-faced nanny who stormed to his rescue—receiving a sharp blow on her head from the kidnapper—and a police officer with a gleaming baton who came onto the scene and chased the kidnapper away.

Piaget finished his story, which he vowed he remembered vividly, with a surprise ending: it never happened! As it turned out, in a death-bed confession many years later, the nanny wrote to Piaget's parents revealing that she had invented the entire story to gain extra privileges from them. In Piaget's memory, the nanny's story had acquired a reality of its own. He fully believed it for a good part of his life. Indeed, over the years, the tale became further filled in with colorful images and details that Piaget unintentionally invented in his own mind.

Piaget's message to our seminar was that our memories are partly *constructions* that are influenced by thoughts and feelings we have after the events took place. As such, memories are very loosely connected to what actually happened. Some memories, as in the story Piaget told us, may be entirely fictionalized. Some contain details that did not exist in the original event; others omit details that did exist at the time.

None of this implies intentional distortion. To say that memory is a construction simply means that, in recalling events, we can't rely on our mental pictures to be as sharp as snapshots. We patch together whatever approximate images we retain, along with feelings and understandings that shape how we end up perceiving those images. Sometimes the results of this mental construction produce reasonably full and accurate accounts of past events. Other times, we may go blank. Still other times, we get things wrong. Frequently, there remains mystery attached to whether or not a particular recollection has grounding in reality. *Was the house of my rich childhood friend really as palatial as I remember it being? Did I see my mother crying when her sister died, or do I just remember her that way because I know now she suffered a great loss? Did my first-grade teacher actually smack my knuckles with a ruler when I talked in class, or is this just something that I once read about teachers doing back then?*

Years on, I think back to Piaget's message as I try to understand my own mental muddle about my father before my recent discoveries. It seems likely that some informative clues about him and his whereabouts must have slipped out of the mouths of the grown-ups around me from time to time. Yet my memory retains few trace of such clues. Did I hear some things that I ignored or quickly forgot? Were some things mentioned that I did not want to hear? Did I know things that I did not know I knew? Or that I misunderstood at the time, or that I later misremembered?

Reclaiming Old Memories and Piercing the Bubble of Obliviousness

I recall one early clue that came by way of an insult from a particularly nasty lady who had a grievance against me because I failed to do a chore she had requested of me. When I called her to apologize, she said, "Well, the apple doesn't fall far from the tree, does it?" This insult, of course, implied that my father was equally unreliable, and had I been paying attention, I might have grasped the implication that he "went missing" of his own accord rather than as a casualty of war. But if my memory is right—always an uncertain proposition—I had no inkling of what the insult meant when she said it. The lady's insult fell on deaf ears; the idea that I was similar to my missing father in some unfavorable way did not register. But her insult did not simply go in one ear and out the other: after all these years I still remember what she said. Why would I remember her unpleasant string of words unless I did have some intimation that she was hitting a nerve?

In this and other instances, my obliviousness to clues must have come from my need for self-preservation and positive development. I may have made no effort to understand that lady's insult because even then I had a sense of the powerful influence of father-son identification, an influence that can support or detract from a child's own efforts to build a positive identity. The initial building blocks of personal identity, as Erikson wrote, are the childhood identifications that develop out of early relationships with admired people such as mothers and fathers—and for a boy, especially his father. In adolescence the childhood identifications are sorted through, added to, and eventually integrated in a self-constructed personal identity that guides the person's path forward. The early childhood identifications don't determine the ultimate character of a person's identity, but they do provide some of the original material for it; thus their nature remains of consequence.

In my case, I must have instinctively felt a need to block out information about my father that would lead me toward undesirable childhood identifications. I wanted to avoid anything that could distract me from my efforts to grow up in a commendable way, to pursue a destiny I could be proud of, to get on and stay on a path to success. I did not want to learn anything about a father who might prove to be less than honorable. I did not need a negative role model.

It was not until I conducted my recent life review that I figured this out. Any life review must reckon with the influence of parents and other role models, either present or absent. It must explore the ways in which our identities may have been shaped by our early relationships and by our chosen reactions to those relationships. This is exactly what my life review accomplished in helping me understand the roots and meaning of my aversion to information about my father and his whereabouts.

The aversion persisted throughout much of my life. It obscured whatever fragments of information about my father might have crossed my mental radar screen during childhood and adolescence. The first time I was able to digest news that my father survived the war was during that awkward conversation with my mother when I was in college. In her brief visit to my college dorm, she mentioned that she had been receiving a modest amount of child support from him (I recall the number as $100 per month, by no means a reliable recollection). My mother had not been contributing to my college expenses, so she felt she should share the child support money with me.

My memory is clear about my reactions to my mother's disclosure—and, looking back, with the perspective of my life review, I can now see that my reactions were revealing. I did not feel surprised to learn that my father was still alive. I was uninterested in my mother's contacts with my father over child support or any other matter. What I remember most vividly is that I felt embarrassed by my mother's implicit admission that she had hidden the real facts of my father's disappearance from me during my entire childhood.

My mother did not share my sense of awkwardness. She made her statement in a matter-of-fact, detached manner. I was perturbed by her manner but touched by the generosity of her offer, since she was scraping by with limited resources. I refused it with murmured thanks. The entire conversation probably lasted less than a minute.

In retrospect, my lack of surprise at my mother's disclosure suggests to me that I already knew more about my father's existence than I consciously realized. Perhaps some clues that may have popped up from time to time during my childhood and early adolescence had penetrated my understanding in some inchoate way. Perhaps I had heard other information about him, now lost to my memory, which I ignored out of fear or indifference but which had left a trace of dormant cognizance. What information could this have been? Did someone (my mother, my grandmother) once tell me that my father would like to meet me if I wanted? Or was this just a wish, a fantasy, a dream of mine? I rack my brain to pin this down but come up empty.

Mostly, I recall the discomfort I felt during that conversation with my mother. She lived another forty-two years, and we never discussed the matter again.

My Close and Distant Mother

The relationship between a single mother and her only child is bound to be intense and filled with perplexing feelings. No doubt the mental fog that long obscured my understanding of what happened to my father stemmed in part from the emotional tangles of my childhood with my mother. Her own strong personality added a heightened intensity to the difficult parenting situation she was left in when my father did not return.

Describing my mother in an objective way may not be possible for me, but the life story that I needed to construct demanded that I take a shot at it. With the distance of the decade and a half since her death, I can note some things about her that others who knew her might agree with, which at least is some approximation of objectivity.

At age three, my mother lost her father to a disease that was never diagnosed because he did not have money for a doctor. Her own mother, devastated and less than competent, left her and her brother in the care of their uncle and aunt, Louis and Esther. Both Louis and Esther were children of European immigrants who came to this country penniless and then struggled against the hardships of very limited means. Thrift was the defining element of their family culture. One oft-repeated story was Esther's determination to keep her winter coat wearable for thirty years by constantly mending it.

My mother was smart and stylish by strength of will, but she had no financial assets and not much education. At twenty-one, she moved to New York City to study fashion design. There, she met twenty-year-old Army sergeant Philip Damon, who was on a brief leave from his wartime post in Europe. She quickly married Philip and got pregnant, not necessarily in that order. (New York City records note their marriage date as February 26, 1944; I was born eight and a half months after that.) Soon after they wed, Philip returned to the battlefront, never to see my mother again. My mother returned home to her Uncle Louis and Aunt Esther in preparation for my arrival on the scene.

I have been able to retrieve one small but striking document from my father's own hand after he returned from his New York visit with my mother to his wartime service on the front. It was a notification he sent my mother in the summer of 1944, reporting that his military division was the 135th Signal Radio Intelligence Corps. He addressed the notification to the address of Uncle Louis and Aunt Esther, the home where my mother was living.

My father's notification to my mother, the one trace of him she retained for her remaining sixty-two years, began, *"Dear Pie-Face."* Was

From:

To:
Mrs Philip A. Damon, Jr

400 West Elm St

Brockton, Mass

Philip A. Damon, Jr
11113919

See Instruction No. 2   (Sender's complete address above)

DEAR   Pie-Face   :

PLEASE ADDRESS ME AS SHOWN BELOW UNTIL OTHERWISE ADVISED.

Sgt   Philip   A.   Damon, Jr.   11113919
(Grade)   (First name)   (Initial)   (Last name)   (Army serial number)

135th Sig RADIO INTELLIGENCE CO
(Company, battery, etc.)   (Regiment, group, or other organization.)

APO No. 887   , % Postmaster, NY, NY

The above COMPLETE ADDRESS should be placed on ALL MAIL sent to me.   MY CODE

CABLE ADDRESS IS

Normal signature   Philip Damon Jr

NOTE.—Newspapers and magazines may need your old address for correct processing. When
advising publishers of change of address, complete the following:

My old address was

V-MAIL

Dear Pie-Face

this a common 1940s salutation of affection? Or was it an intimate joke between the two? At the bottom was my father's signature, the only one I have.

I found this document lying at the bottom of my mother's desk drawer when I cleared out her belongings after her death. No other signs of him existed in any of the places she had lived as an adult. Among all the remembrances of my father that she might have held on to—photos, letters, gifts—this single note remained over all the decades that passed since her brief time with him. Today, when I glance at that sparse notification on a bureaucratic army form, I am brought close to tears.

The adjectives that most readily come to mind when I think of my mother are bright, caring, critical, and committed. She loved art and fashion, which became her vocation. As a young and middle-aged woman, she was considered attractive by men (a number of whom, for reasons I could never fathom, made a point of remarking on this to me). Yet she never remarried. My conjecture about this is simple: she was quite hard to get along with.

Although volatile of mood, my mother could be counted on to fulfill her responsibilities. Instead of a marriage partner, she had two objects of devotion. One of them was me, to my good fortune (after all, there was no one else to look after me when I was young). The other was the Catholic Church. In the Church, she found solace when my father abandoned her and a sense of meaning for all the hard things that life threw at her. Her faith provided her with hope for a better world here and in the afterlife. She found animated and caring relationships with a steady stream of devoted priests over her eighty-four-year lifetime. They became her religious guides, her loyal friends, her intellectual sparring partners, and, in a slightly psychological sense, proxies for the father she lost when she was three and the husband she lost when she was twenty-three.

After the war and for the remainder of the 1940s, my mother waited in vain for my father to come back. I've been able to reconstruct evidence of this sad time in her life through a search of the archives of the *Berkshire Eagle*, the hometown newspaper of Pittsfield, Massachusetts,

Mother and infant me in 1945, waiting for end of war and return of Dad

the small city where my father's family was living. The *Eagle* posted notices of three visits from "Mrs. Helen Damon and her son William" to "the home of Philip A. and Ruth Van Buren Damon" during the period from 1945 through 1948. (It now amazes me that any newspaper, even a local one, would bother to record such family visits: this might say something about the status of the Damons in Pittsfield, about journalism in that era, or perhaps both.) I have no distinct recollection of those visits, although I do retain a blurry mental image of my grandfather lying sick in his bed during what likely was my final visit at age four. That one image sits alone in my mind, unaccompanied by any surrounding details. Our visits to the Damon family home ended in 1948, when it must have become evident to my mother that waiting for my father's return was hopeless.

At that point, at the end of the 1940s, my mother had something of a breakdown. I found out about this only recently, after I had begun my life review and the investigations it required. I contacted a person who might know about this period, my mother's cousin Gerry, who lost a leg fighting in France during the war. Gerry was still alive and mentally alert but was in fact on the verge of a decline into dementia, and he would die soon after. Like many others who have played a part in this story, Gerry came through for me in the nick of time during his final months. He told me that my mother was "completely devastated" when she realized my father had no intention of returning to her. She "went away" to some nearby place in Massachusetts to recover. He guessed it must have been a mental health retreat of some sort, but he wasn't sure.

My mother's disappointment over my father's refusal to return was so severe that for the rest of her life she never could trust any seeming good fortune. She always retained a suspicion that things would turn out badly in the end. Even when things were looking good, she was convinced there would be an eventual reversal of fortune, and so she guarded herself against any expression of optimism. In part, this represented a stoic determination to face reality in all its toughness. There was a superstitious element to it too: if you blindly believed things were going to go well, you were bound to get hit with bad luck.

She passed this guardedness along to me—another indirect legacy of my father. The sense of dread that something could go wrong in the end, no matter how good things looked at present, was communicated to me as a child on the occasion of every propitious event in either of our lives. Whenever joys came our way, vigilance was need to guard them.

One striking finding from child development research is that children who feel abandoned by either parent at an early age develop an enduring dread of nonexistence. Erikson wrote about this as a problem in "basic trust." Without basic trust early on, it's a constant challenge to keep a grip on the endurance and continuity of your own existence.

He wrote that the foundations of basic trust are established in the course of secure parent-child relations. Research on the importance of "secure attachment" between caregiver and child has confirmed Erikson's clinical intuitions.

Life reviews can draw upon such insights from child development theory and research. Although everyone's life story is unique, some patterns in human development are common to many persons. The relation between secure attachment in the early years and later basic trust is one of these patterns. Knowing this can help those with tendencies toward being excessively wary and guarded to place such tendencies in perspective with similar patterns among people who have had disrupted or missing relationships with parents during childhood. This removes elements of self-blame in ascribing causes for such tendencies; it also suggests remediation strategies such as intentionally building stable relationships that emanate trust. In drawing upon general knowledge of human development, life reviews can provide similar analyses for any troubling dispositions that have arisen from the early experiences that the review has uncovered.

As I reviewed my life, I uncovered many things that I had missed and had to struggle to make up for. Basic trust fell within that category. Learning more about exactly what was missing in my childhood, understanding how and why it was missing, and coming to terms with it, have been a help to me in readdressing basic trust at this time in my life. It has provided me with new tools for managing an old struggle.

I rarely welcome struggles in my life, yet looking back I can see that certain struggles were certainly good for me, because compensating for shortfalls can lead to the development of new capacities. When I was in sixth grade, I was cut from a school baseball team without a fair tryout because another boy's father knew the coach well. I had no father to make my case. I was forced to figure out how to work up righteous steam on my own behalf and insist on a fairer tryout. As a result, I was granted an equal share of playing time during the season. It was not a total victory, not quite fair (because the other kid was really incompetent), but it did provide me with a lesson in how to stick up for myself. Over the course of multiple similar incidents, self-reliance became part of my personal tool kit. It was a developmental compensation for life without a father.

My mother died in 2006 at age eighty-four, felled by a rapidly metastasizing brain tumor that mercifully caused her little suffering. To the end, she was stoic and steely. She also kept her anger alive until her final breath. She was furious when she was moved to an assisted care room that had no space for her cherished collection of dresses. I arranged for her three grandchildren to make separate visits to see her. She loved them dearly, and the visits meant the world to her. But she spent time during each visit scolding the visiting grandchild for whatever sins of commission or omission she believed him or her to be guilty of. This was the way she chose to go out, in the same manner we all knew well. Another mixed blessing, with its own special share of challenges and developmental compensations.

2

Life Stories

WE TELL STORIES about ourselves all the time. Sometimes we tell stories about ourselves to other people. Sometimes we tell stories about ourselves to ourselves. In either case, our stories say something about who we are, who we would like to be, and how we would like to be seen. Our life stories are ways of building, presenting, and confirming the identities that have given us meaning and direction in life.

Life stories can range from the dramatic to the ordinary. We might tell a high-stakes story about a time we took a gallant risk for a noble cause, such as rescuing a drowning child from an ocean tide or pulling someone out of a burning building. Or we might tell a more everyday tale about a hard day at the office or a shopping coup while bargain hunting. We might recount a lengthy saga of suffering, struggle, and triumph. Or we might share a brief account of an enjoyable trip we took on vacation. In each case, though, the story will tell us, and others, something about ourselves.

When we tell our life stories, we usually are not aware of their identity-presenting agenda. Other goals that coexist with self-presentation seem more obvious to us. The stories we tell others may be intended to entertain, to amuse, to influence, or even possibly to deceive. The stories we tell ourselves may be intended to remind us about incidents we've treasured and now enjoy reliving, or to help us rethink events we have found disturbing in the past and now wish to resolve in our present thoughts. But along with these other goals, whether intended or not, any story we tell about ourselves conveys information about who we are and who we want to be.

Depending on how committed we are to honesty—and how good our memories are—our stories vary widely in their accuracy. Rarely are we able to tell a story that's "the whole truth and nothing but the truth." We are selective in the events and details that we choose to convey, and we don't always get those events and details exactly right. The inaccuracies in our life stories occur not necessarily because we are trying to deceive ourselves or others (although sometimes people do that), but more commonly because our information is incomplete. We may not know all the facts about an incident we are trying to recall, we may have memory lapses, or we may have false memories that include imaginary embellishments. Life stories are not complete accounts of what happened on any given occasion. Our life stories are incomplete in other ways as well. If it's an ongoing story (as are most life stories, other than deathbed confessions), we can't know how it will end.

Whatever we perceive to be the reasons for our stories, and whatever degree of accuracy we may achieve, our storytelling continues as long as we remain alive. Each day offers us new opportunities to revisit our understanding of who we are and to forge stronger, more authentic, and more life-affirming identities. The life stories that we tell ourselves permit us to do this—especially if we go about telling them in an intentional way.

Life stories enable us to make sense of events that seem meaningless or dispiriting if just left alone to fester. They help us salvage benefits from our regrets. One saving grace of the human condition is our capacity to find meaning in life's most painful occurrences. Stories that place regrettable incidents in the context of what we have learned from them can help us do this.

A thoughtful story can help us find meaning in events that otherwise may seem random or disconnected. It can weave our life events into a coherent narrative about who we've been and who we hope to become.

It can help us connect the past with the present and prepare us for the future we'd like to have. In this way, stories about who we've been and who we are can help us deal with the inevitable challenges life throws at us. They give us agency in determining who we shall become. Storytelling is a fundamental human capacity, and life stories are a prime way that humans bring coherence and positivity to their life experiences. Any life story, whether lengthy or brief, offers us a chance to review some portion of our lives and, with that, a chance to reflect on who we are.

Take, for example, our sense of how we've acted in important relationships. For most of us, relations with parents play a large role in our life stories. We would like to think of ourselves as good children who have been loved by our parents, who have made our parents proud, who have expressed gratitude for whatever our parents have given us, and who have always been there for our parents until the very end. This ideal, however, is rarely achieved.

It is common, for example, to feel we should have devoted more time to a sick or dying parent, no matter how much we manage to do. People with dying parents tend to be in midlife, with many competing responsibilities, such as jobs, families, and community engagements. It is hard be in more than one place at once, so we may feel forced to balance obligations. Although we have tried to do our best for our parents, looking back often uncovers a residue of guilt: Could I have stayed at my mother's bedside longer? Should I have said things to her, or done things for her, that I never quite got around to? As unjustified or irrational as such feelings may be, they can leave a legacy of distress and doubt. A new narrative account of the whole relationship over time can trigger a process of reflective review that resolves such feelings by recasting them in a more forgiving light.

Similarly, many of us may feel that we've had troubling conflicts—with work colleagues, old romantic partners, former friends, or relatives—that were never adequately resolved. We may still feel nagging insecurities about these relationships and regret over not making things right. If there is still the opportunity, with careful reflection we might now find a chance to do so. If not, we at least could figure out what went wrong, learn from it, and recognize the mistakes we have made. Ultimately, such recognition bears on our identity, our sense of how we've conducted our important relationships.

This is where a deliberate and intentional approach to storytelling can come in. Troubling imperfections in our past behaviors are central to some stories, but these are not the only stories available to us. Just as there are things to regret in virtually every relationship, there also are things to value and treasure. Revising a troubling story to achieve a fairer balance between what we wish we might have changed and what we have cherished can go a long way toward placing life's inevitable regrets in a broader perspective that conveys an overall sense of positivity and gratitude. A deliberate and intentional approach to life stories, such as a life review of the sort that I describe in this book, offers a way to *affirm* our life experiences rather than rue or despair them.

In the field of psychology, the groundbreaking promotor of an affirmative approach was Victor Frankl, a major influence on the views I present in this book. Frankl wrote his landmark *Man's Search for Meaning* while imprisoned in a concentration camp during World War II. His book ushered in a new perspective on how to promote psychological well-being that emphasizes purpose, meaning, and other elevated human capacities. Frankl's insights became the foundation of now-prevalent trends in psychology that focus on the value of positive mental states.

It's worth noting that Frankl gave his book a different title from the one eventually crafted by its English-language translator. Frankl's original title was *Nevertheless Say Yes to Life*—capturing, in a short phrase, what *affirming* our past experiences means. Affirmation of past choices and events that have shaped our lives means saying *yes* rather than *no* to them. It means looking for lessons in mistakes. It means finding opportunity in hardships and redemption in regrets. Frankl showed how this could be done under the bleakest of circumstances.

The benefits of affirmation have been recognized in popular culture as well. A lyric by Johnny Mercer goes: "You've got to accentuate the positive / eliminate the negative / and latch on to the affirmative." Another famous song reminds us to stay "on the sunny side of the street," and there has been well-known guidance about "making lemonade out of lemons." But when life inflicts really hard blows, such advice is easier given than followed. The difficult question is, How can we do this through all the numerous ups and downs of a lifetime?

The field of psychology has offered answers to this question, based on Frankl's work and on the recent "positive psychology" approach that followed his lead. My thinking has been influenced by these insightful approaches, and my deliberations in this book reflect that; but these approaches are not the primary focus of this book. Rather, this book focuses on my use of a *life-review* approach that has emerged from the fields of psychiatry, personality psychology, and narrative research. Nevertheless, it should be clear that my use of the life-review approach is directed squarely at the affirmation objective championed by Frankl and pursued in research and practice by the positive psychology movement.

Affirming our past experiences means finding the constructive outcomes they've brought. Even the most difficult times can lead to learning, character growth, new opportunities, and other personal benefits. It is true that some events are so catastrophic that we must mourn them: living in this world can be excruciatingly tragic. But as long as our minds are intact, we have the chance to find meaning in our experiences. The first place to look is at ourselves. Whatever happened in the past, we would not be the same people we are now if those things had not happened. For this reason, knowing and accepting our identities means affirming rather than denying the choices and events that took us here. This is why telling life stories in a manner that provides affirmation of our pasts helps us build fulfilling identities that look to our future directions with hope.

Life stories can help us come to terms with problematic past experiences of many kinds. People often are troubled by opportunities they've missed. A student decides to take a gap year rather than apply to medical school and then loses the chance to go to medical school after suffering a permanently disabling accident while traveling during that year. A manager leaves a secure position at a large corporation in order to start the restaurant of his dreams, and eventually the restaurant fails. An investor is offered a chance to buy Amazon stock at pennies a share when it first comes out but declines because he considers it too risky. Career and money matters abound with these kinds of mishaps. Stories that turn a positive light on such realities can help us accept these kinds of misfortunes, placing them in perspective with the more auspicious moments that our lives as a whole have enjoyed. Stories that extract lessons from mistakes we have made help us avoid similar mistakes going forward.

With deliberation, stories of regret can be turned into affirmative stories reflecting self-forgiveness, appreciation, and feelings of satisfaction. Such stories can capture the entire reality of our experiences, the good along with the bad. They enable us to build robust senses of identity that bestow confidence in our abilities to cope with unexpected further challenges.

There are times when reassessments of identity are especially called for. Graduation from high school or college often triggers a search for purposes that can galvanize our energies and carry us into adult life. In the process, we may find ourselves reexamining our fundamental sense of who we are. A commitment to a long-term relationship such as marriage is another such time. As we contemplate merging our life paths, our homes, and our finances with another person's, this may prompt deeper reflections on how we have come to this juncture and where it will take us. Conversely, the end of a marriage through death or divorce can cause a disruption in our sense of who we are. A story that has been built around the "we" of that relationship now must change to find a new focus. When children grow up and leave home, parents are compelled to rethink the role that has defined a central component of their identities. Who will we be now, when the shape of our day-to-day lives no longer bends around our children's needs? Retirement from a job poses the same challenge, as does a career change. Our vocational stories are woven into our senses of identity, and it can be difficult to untangle the two. Health events—a cancer diagnosis, an injury, a decline in important physical abilities—also affect us in ways that reach beyond the physical. A personal identity anchored in physical capacities and activities must shift. An athlete who can no longer run, a pianist whose fingers become frozen with arthritis, a woman growing past the age of childbearing, indeed every one of us who advances across any irreversible threshold of aging must find new life stories that are no longer predicated on the capacities we have lost.

Every transition poses junctures, where a life can branch off in one direction or another. After graduation, a young person might choose to take a job immediately, to go on to further schooling, to see the world, to enter a monastery for spiritual growth, to enlist in military service, or to take any number of other possible paths. Any choice will foreclose, or at least delay, other options, which then become the "roads not taken." As we look back, it is almost inevitable that we will wonder what our lives would be like if we had taken a different road. We naturally would like to understand how the turning points in our lives shaped who we are now and who we will become. We wish to be at peace with the directions that our lives took as a consequence of the choices we made.

The retelling of life stories can lead the way forward. Part of the appeal of gatherings such as high-school and college reunions is that they invite this kind of storytelling. In a less immediate manner, so do social media outlets such as Facebook. When we "catch up" with old friends, we reexamine and reconstruct our identities. As we tell our stories to one another, or as we display photos illustrating small pieces of our stories, we see how our lives have been going. We question why we've ended up where we have, and we speculate about what comes next.

For each of our life transitions, and for other times in the course of our development, the telling of life stories puts us in touch with our established identities and provides guidance for the future that is based on accounts of who we've been in the past. As we encounter difficulties and experience regrets, revised life stories offer us ways of setting promising new directions.

This is something that people do spontaneously, often without realizing it, in response to the ups and downs that every life brings and the developmental challenges that all people share. Identity building is a universal psychological task, and the stories people tell about themselves are the standard means of performing this task. The utility of such spontaneous storytelling may be amplified by bringing intentional reflections to the effort. The life-review approach, though fairly new and relatively unexplored, offers one promising avenue for facilitating this kind of intentional reflection.

The Life Review

In the fields of psychiatry and psychology, there's an approach to telling stories about ourselves that is not widely known, despite its potential for building a positive identity reflecting a spirit of affirmation. The approach has been called, variously, "life review," "guided autobiography," "reminiscence," "narrative identity," or other similar terms that denote reflective examinations of the choices and events that make up a life. The approach entails examining one's memories of the past and bringing these to bear on one's present thoughts and feelings, one's sense of self, and one's future hopes and expectations. It offers a way of making sense of our lives in a hopeful and affirmative manner.

The life-review method was pioneered by Robert Butler, a legendary psychiatrist who was concerned with the problem of depression in aging patients. Butler believed that the depressive symptoms of his patients stemmed from the aimless way they remembered their pasts.

He devised a procedure for helping people conduct "life reviews" that highlighted the key purposes they had pursued in previous periods of their lives. By finding the positive products of their earlier experiences—including those that may have appeared unfortunate at the time—Butler believed that people could affirm the value of their lives and chart a hopeful path forward. He wrote, "One's life does not have to have been a 'success' in the popular sense of the word. People take pride in a feeling of having done their best . . . and sometimes from simply having survived against terrible odds."

Before he was able to fully develop this method, Butler moved on to a celebrated career in gerontology. He founded the National Institute of Aging and wrote a Pulitzer Prize–winning book on successful aging. In his public role, it was Butler who coined the term "ageism." But he never found the time to return to his innovative life-review idea before his 2007 death. Late in his life, Butler wrote that he regretted not having that time, because he believed the idea would prove useful for all people in the search for ways to live maximally meaningful lives—whether or not battling depression, and whether old or young.

Butler believed that reflective life reviews would promote "intellectual and personal growth, and wisdom" throughout the life span. "The life review," he wrote, "should be recognized as a necessary and healthy process in daily life as well as a useful tool in the mental health care of older people." Among the psychological benefits he noted were the resolution of old conflicts; an optimistic view of one's future; "a sense of serenity, pride in accomplishment"; a "feeling of having done one's best"; a capacity to enjoy present pleasures such as humor, love, nature, and contemplation; and "a comfortable acceptance of the life cycle, the universe, and the generations." This, of course, is a compelling list of the main pillars of psychological health.

Approaches similar to the life review have been used in psychological science to examine well-being during childhood and adolescence, adult personality development, and problems such as recovery from trauma and reform after criminality. The pioneering research of Dan

McAdams and his colleagues at Northwestern University employed a "life-story interview" that they devised to study identity growth in the adult years. McAdams's life-story interview method and his method for conducting "guided autobiographies" with his research subjects are the most systematic and rigorous scientific instruments for examining life reminiscences I know.

Based on his studies, McAdams created a powerful theory of personality that posited a culminating "level 3" grounded in life stories that bestow unity and meaning in a person's identity. McAdams has written about the importance of generativity in forming a mature identity and about the value of "redemptive" thinking in salvaging benefits from negative events and experiences. Although my focus in this book is more attuned to the idiosyncratic twists and turns of one individual's development than to the general personality patterns that are revealed through McAdams's structured methods, I have learned much from his methods and theory. In addition, McAdams's insights about *generativity* and *redemption* have contributed to my understanding of the closely related concepts of *purpose* and *compensation* that are at the heart of this book.

McAdams's work has inspired a string of studies on narrative identity in childhood and adolescence. The theory of narrative identity posits that identity formation can be promoted by creating a life story that integrates past and present experiences with future aspirations. Purpose plays a key role in the narrative identity approach, which assumes that purposeful aspirations are central to well-constructed life stories. Research using storytelling methods with adolescents has shown benefits for the research subjects ranging from improved narrative skills to higher levels of psychological well-being. This suggestive research also has made preliminary inroads into the possible relationship between personal storytelling and the capacity to have a productive and meaningful life.

Gerontologist James Birren studied the uses of autobiographical life reviews in work with small community groups. Birren concluded that life reviews not only can increase insight about one's past but also can prepare one for the inevitable changes over time that life brings. Birren and his colleagues guided people's autobiographies toward the following life themes: (1) turning points that resulted in a person taking a particular direction, (2) the history of the person's family, (3) the person's work or career, (4) the role that money has played, (5) the role that health and body have played, (6) romantic and sexual experiences, (7) experience with loss and death, and (8) beliefs and values that give meaning to the person's life.

Birren identified an impressive list of personal benefits of life reviews, among which are "recognition of past adaptive strategies and application to current needs . . . reconciliation with the past and resolution of past resentments and negative feelings . . . resurgence of interest in past activities . . . greater sense of meaning in life . . . [and] ability to face the nearing end of life with a feeling that one has contributed to the world." Birren's view is that a life review can be a way to transform past injuries into adaptive strengths. He quotes Hemingway's observation, "The world breaks everyone, but many are stronger at the broken places."

A life review is a "whole person" approach. Everything matters. Anything that a person has experienced, or anticipates experiencing, can be better understood when seen in the context of the person's entire life history and what it has come to mean to that individual. Such an approach stands in stark contrast to academic psychology's tendency to break our activities into little parts and analyze the parts separately. A life review does not try to explain behavior by any one factor or to reduce a person's choices to any one cause. All of life counts—past, present, and future.

Life reviews can be useful at any age, beginning in adolescence, when young people start to sift through their reminiscences for the initial building blocks of their self-identities, and later in adulthood, when people revise their identities in ways informed by experience in the world.

A life review begins with determining the actual facts of one's life, to the full extent that this is possible. This means retrieving school and employment records, speaking to relatives and old friends about past shared experiences, conducting ancestry searches for information about one's parents and their forebears, and engaging in rigorous examinations of memories to try to sort out any illusions from what really happened. Journals, letters, emails, and social media posts all can play a part in this endeavor.

An Unexpected Journey

Like many in my active, youth-oriented cohort, I let my midlife years slide by with no particular concern—much like the line in the Paul Simon song about "stringing one more year on the line." I felt no urge to look backward, no need for questioning the long-standing life story I had been telling myself.

That story included the loss of a father I never met and knew nothing about while I was growing up. As a child, whenever anyone would ask me where my father was, I'd blurt out that catchphrase my mother had given me: "He was missing in World War II." It was like a mantra that deterred conscious reflection on my part and further questioning on the part of my listener. This answer usually evoked sympathy, although the sympathy seemed curious and misplaced to me at that time. I was making my way through childhood, doing OK, enjoying my youth, certainly not feeling sorry for myself. I was so in the dark about my loss of a father and how it happened that the notion that I could be lacking something beneficial never dawned on me. My obliviousness had the upside of preventing me from feeling dejected and losing my youthful hopefulness and lofty aspirations. But, as I've now realized, it also led me to deny my real feelings and neglect shortcomings that I should have addressed.

Then, not long before I turned sixty-five, my understanding of my family history, my sense of my own past, and my beliefs about how and why I took the paths I did while growing up were rocked by the consequential call from my daughter that uncovered the real story of my father's disappearance. My obliviousness and denials of my life's true story came to an end.

Robert Butler commented, "Emotional events in a family, such as the loss of a loved one through war, can leave a profound mark. Such events may be concealed as family secrets but then resurface unexpectedly through the process of life review." For me, of course, it was not an in-progress life review that uncovered the secret; it was the uncovering of the secret that inspired a life review. It was while confronting the discovery of my father's story that I became drawn to the idea of conscious revision of my own identity story. My discoveries became first the trigger and then a large part of the life review I undertook—a process that gave me a new fix on who I am and where I am heading.

The new and more accurate story that I worked to compose altered my understanding of my past. It raised fundamental questions about how, in the absence of a father, I established my identity and life purposes—and, inevitably, questions about *what might have been different* had I known him.

Questions like this can be destabilizing, in the way that discovering a new fossil can upset theories about evolutionary links among species. New and unsettling information during any period of life can lead to pain, to growth, or to both together. In my case, the information that I discovered has become part of the personal integrating effort that marked my own ultimate quest for affirmation versus despair. The recently discovered truths that upended my knowledge of my life course have elements of pain and letdown, but also redeeming elements of unexpected courage and decency. It is a story of wartime, a time when people can be thrown into the air like confetti, landing wherever they are blown.

As Butler had predicted, the resurfacing of family secrets in my life awakened in me a need for renewed self-examination. My intuitions told me that the life-review approach could facilitate the essential quest for the authentic identity that people of all ages seek. Along with my personal interest in examining my own life, my professional interest also was triggered. I was curious to see how a life review oriented to positive themes such as purpose and gratitude might foster life affirmation, identity growth, and their psychological benefits.

In Search of Ego Integrity

The idea of a life review has a special appeal for people moving into their later adulthood years. At that time, it's natural to explore the meaning of our lives by reflecting on where we've come from, where we've been, where we are now, and where we wish to end up. It's a time for summing up and for thinking anew about how best to spend our remaining years. In this effort, we can use life stories to revise and revitalize our personal identities and the purposes that flow from them. A life review offers an intentional way to choose and tell the life stories that can help us do this. It offers a way to integrate these stories into a coherent narrative that affirms our past and guides our future.

Life reviews require looking backward at the past, sideways in the present, and forward to the future, and then integrating what we have come up with into a coherent vision that makes sense. This vision will include everything that's given meaning to a life: core values, significant relationships, contributions and achievements, spiritual faith, and well-examined stories of where we came from, how we got to where we are now, and where we hope we will be heading.

The work of integrating the past, present, and future dimensions of our life stories into a coherent vision is what makes possible the sense of integrity that brings serenity and satisfaction. The shared lexical roots of *integrating* and *integrity* are not accidental. Any effort at integration hinges on coming to terms with the past, *because the past is an integral part of who we are.* As Faulkner wrote in *Requiem for a Nun*, "The past is never dead. It's not even past."

Understanding the past is a necessary step in this quest. In addition, present realities and future aspirations also must be understood, accepted, and integrated into an affirmative account of one's life. Fully mature integrity combines all the times of one's life into a coherent whole. Past, present, and future selves then merge with ease.

There may be (indeed, probably will be) discrepancies between the ways we have acted at different ages. Certainly there will be variations in how we experienced life over the years. But an integrated self sees such variations as part of an evolving narrative, rather than as violations of our beliefs and commitments—or, worse, as negations of our fundamental reasons for being.

The backward, sideways, and forward looks that constitute an integrated summing-up of a life eventually lose their distinct temporal significance: the experience of integration transcends the separate time periods. In a successfully integrated moment, it feels as if the looks across time are happening all at once. Not only is the past "not even past"; the future too becomes part of the present, and the present is seen as moving into the future.

The great psychologist Erik Erikson called this process a journey toward "ego integrity." The key to this journey is finding threads that connect the circumstances we've been given (our family situations, our genetic and biological statuses, our social and cultural backgrounds) with conditions we have created for ourselves through choices we've made and actions we've taken.

The journey toward ego integrity offers closure, fulfillment, and a contentment based on the conviction that our lives have been as well lived as possible under the circumstances that we've been given. Even in the face of catastrophic life outcomes, we at least can say that we have tried our best with what we had to work with. Erikson considered this conviction to be a culminating wisdom, an "informed and detached concern with life itself even in the face of death itself."

Ultimately, this means accepting the lives we've been given, in all their jaggedness, and recognizing that both our best and our worst times on this earth are transient. Failing to take this journey risks regret over missed opportunities, a belief that one's life has been misspent, and an abiding despair that can dampen one's remaining years.

The journey toward ego integrity requires an understanding of where we've come from, where we went from there, why we made the choices that shaped our destinies, and what sorts of persons we have become. This is a "mirror test" with historical dimensions. Little wonder that as people advance through the mid and later periods of development, many become intrigued by the ancestral influences that gave them their start.

Conversations That Could Have Been

In each of our pasts, it was our parents who launched us on our voyages and set our initial courses, for better or worse. Everything that follows bears their marks: their biological, ideational, and relational legacies. This is a central reason why, sooner or later, we often yearn to know as much as possible about who our parents really were. This is just as true for those of us who never knew one or both of our parents as it is for those who grew up in stable nuclear families.

If you outlive your parents by several years, the time likely will come when you'll wish you could speak with them at least once again. You may have questions about what happened in their lives that only they would be able to answer or questions about your own early life. Maybe you will wish you could talk to them about things that did not occur to you while they were alive. You may have feelings you never got around to expressing, or your feelings may have changed and you would like a chance to let them know that. There could be a legacy of misunderstanding, or gratitude never expressed, or resentment that you failed to acknowledge and resolve when they were alive. But it is as if someone clicked on "permanently delete" during some computer work and there is no recover function for that program. Life is that sort of program, and death is a deletion that we can't reverse. Other than on the level of spiritual beliefs and practices (prayers, flowers on graves, dreams, séances), death closes down conversations: it's the ultimate disruption that ends every relationship sooner or later.

Our insights about our families mature too slowly for us to know what we have missed in crucial conversations that never took place. Some people with strong perceptive insights manage to get closure on important issues during or just before deathbed conversations. But even they often experience a desire to reconstitute the relationship one more time. A sense of completion always remains elusive, and the hunger for completion grows stronger as we come to realize how elusive it is.

For those in family relationships that were close and fulfilling, the impossibility of post-death communications may spur occasional feelings of sadness and longing. For those in family relationships that were troubled and never set right, their feelings after a death can be complicated enough to lead to years of residual confusion and regrets. Sorting out such feelings has been the stuff of psychotherapy from its earliest Freudian days.

And there are some of us with even higher stakes in the game. For those of us who grew up never knowing a mother or father, the urge to communicate with the missing parent can be intense; and if that parent has passed away, the frustration of realizing that this is now impossible can be even more intense. In our uncertain world, there are many who lose one or both parents early on, in some cases, even before any relationship began. A parent can disappear from a child's life for a host of reasons: accident or illness, divorce, abandonment, an economic reversal, a forced resettlement, or the countless human dice tosses that come out of revolutions and wars. Children may lose one or both parents forever in such all-too-frequent disturbances. In some cases, a child will have no awareness of how and why it happened, of what that parent was like, or even of who that person actually was.

My mother never remarried, and I remained a boy without a father for the duration of my growing up. As such, my adolescent quest for identity was intensified by needing to find father figures to model on, learn from, and react against—that convoluted mix of endeavors that enables a young person to assemble a stable foundation on which to build a unique sense of self.

As I speak about my own story with friends, it's amazed me how many have told me their own stories of important family members who have gone missing. Wars, financial reversals, and miscellaneous human vices and frailties shuffle the decks often enough for some cards to scatter to the wind. Disrupted family situations and ignorance surrounding them are not as unusual as I once believed when looking around at other families that seemed on the surface more intact than mine. Often, I have found, people in such families express a lingering hunger to get to know, at long last, the missing family member in any way at all, if it still might be possible. As a result of learning my own story, I too felt that hunger.

A fascination with our familial roots can extend far back in our ancestral histories, to our grandparents, great-grandparents, and beyond. In recent years, ancestral archives of every kind have seen rapidly increasing traffic. Large numbers of people now entering their later periods of life have been flocking to the archives to find out as much as they can about their origins and ancestry. The growth of the internet and its powerful search functions have facilitated this surge and contributed to its rapid spread.

Why this hunger to get to know someone who never became an actual part of your life? I believe it's because we are all always on voyages of self-formation, always wishing to check on where we are in our own personal voyage. As long as we retain the mental capacities to examine ourselves, we never stop seeking new answers to questions such as "Where did I come from?" "What am I like?" and "Why am I this way?" We search for answers not only in our own early lives but also in the lives of those in our families who have gone before us.

Beyond our own familial histories, world history too needs to be recalled in order for us to make sense of our own lives. Like personal life stories, shared stories from history also convey identity. Who are we as a people? What have been the historical high points that we should build on? What have been the low points that we should learn to avoid? Which champions should we emulate? Whose mistakes and failures should we know and avoid in the future? Both our past and present selves reflect historical lessons that our forebears have learned, as well as the dramas that we have experienced. In my case, World War II played a special role in the story of my life. It was the event that initially separated me from my father. A major part of the historical past, that colossal war recast my own life at the same time that it transformed the world.

I was born during the final months of that war and have no recollection of that time. My knowledge came from books, movies, history lessons, and tales told to me by older relatives and camp counselors. Until recently, I always thought of that war as an important but remote part of history. Yet, in light of my life review, I have come to understand the way that the war shaped my early experience, my family relationships, my education, and the course of my life. World War II came home to me in a highly personal way, affecting my continuing quest for a coherent life story that could integrate my life history, my present identity, and my future purposes. The past, as Faulkner wrote, is always with us.

Although the past needs to be resolved and integrated into our present and future selves, it must not rule our self-reflections. We need to recognize and consider our past, not get stuck in it. There's an old-world joke that goes something like "I love the past; I hate the present; and I'm fearful of the future." In contrast to this astringent view, we must come to terms with all the time periods we have experienced and integrate them into a coherent account that can provide us with positive directions for our futures.

Doing so requires serious efforts to recapture the events in our past that have shaped us. It also requires us to take new command over those events by construing them in ways that can be helpful to us, now and in the future. As Canadian psychologist Paul Wong has written, "Our past can be both a burden and a resource. The emotional baggage and the scars we carry can sap our energy and reduce our sense of well-being. . . . But the vast reservoir of memories can also serve as a reservoir of wisdom, meaning, and solace." In the chapters that follow, I explore this wide observation in the context of my own quest to unlock my past and the secrets, memories, and revelations that had long been hidden from my awareness.

3

Revisiting Identity
and Purpose

"**LIFE CAN ONLY** be understood backwards," wrote philosopher Søren Kierkegaard in his journal, "but it must be lived forwards." A more contemporary statement of this principle was offered by Steve Jobs at a Stanford University commencement address in June 2005. I was seated on a platform behind Mr. Jobs during his speech, and I could see his blue-jeaned attire that was covered in front by the black robe. I have sat through dozens of commencement addresses in my four decades as a college professor, and I can say without hesitation that this was the most interesting. Midway through the speech, Mr. Jobs shared the following insight: "You can't connect the dots looking forward; you can only connect them looking backward. So you have to trust that the dots will somehow connect in your future."

Kierkegaard and Jobs, each in his own way, captured the key paradox of the life review. Conducting a life review means looking backward at the experiences that have made us who we are today. It offers a way to grasp, as fully and accurately as possible, the core characteristics of our personal identities and how these came to be. This can be a revealing prospect for people interested in making sense of their lives, which includes most people. Yet the true value of a life review does not rest in its retrieval of past history. A life review offers the prospect of renewing present identity in ways that can affirm the present and disclose purposeful directions for the future.

Not all ways of looking back on our lives help much with these goals. Happy memories of sitting in a center seat at a dramatic football game, recollections of a trip to Paris with a meal at a Michelin three-star restaurant, tales of gigantic fish caught during a week at the lake with buddies, reveries of a youthful summer romance, nostalgia for times gone by—all these can be fine fun without carrying significant personal meaning beyond that.

Other ways of looking back can be full of pain and regret: *I could have married my high school sweetheart if I had been bold enough to ask her; I should have helped my friend with his expenses when he was too sick to work; I shouldn't have wasted years of my life trying to be an opera singer when there's so little opportunity in that area; I should have spent more time with my family when my kids were young.* In the classic film *On the Waterfront*, Marlon Brando enacted an iconic example of this way of thinking about the past in his plaintive declaration, "I could have been a contender."

When psychiatrist Robert Butler introduced his life-review method, he stressed that it was not meant to be a random mental walk through a haphazard assortment of recollections. For the goal of building a well-directed identity, some ways of reconstructing the past are more helpful than others. It matters which incidents we recall. The way we think about these incidents matters too. Negative recollections can play an important role, as long as life-affirming lessons are taken from what is recalled. It's not that we should deny or cover up mishaps that cannot be corrected. Some disastrous events in life will require deep and everlasting mourning. But when possible, it is helpful to fully accept our past and present lots in life, to find some value in the mistakes we have made, and to affirm the persons we are now and hope to be in the future.

For a productive life review, it is important to acknowledge our regrets and failures and come to terms with them. Regrets and failures are inevitable in any life. They actually are signs of a vigorous and thoughtful approach to life. If we never failed, it would mean we never tried doing anything challenging. If we never regretted anything, it would mean we never admitted the many mistakes that we all make at one time or another. The problem is not that we have regrets and failures. Rather, the problem is letting recollections of our regrets and failures disturb us endlessly. A life review can help us resolve these and other negative recollections by placing them in contexts that provide our lives with meaning and affirmation. In some cases, as in my own review, this means identifying previously obscured conditions that led to the regrets and failures. In other cases, it means confirming what we've eventually learned from our regrets and failures.

And a life review does not stop with resolving regrets and failures. It places them in the context of an entire life, the life we've been given. It frames the inevitable setbacks that we've encountered in the context of the persons we've now become, the moments of satisfaction we've enjoyed, the relationships we've had, and the contributions we've made to the world at large. It surveys *both* the road not taken *and* the road we ended up on, with a new understanding of how forgoing the first made possible the fruits of the other. It means final acceptance of the paths we have taken. The result is a reformulated identity that opens the way for a confident vision of the road to come.

Continuities and Changes in Personal Identity

A life review produces a coherent narrative out of the countless events and observations that we've experienced over the years. It finds meaningful threads that run through our past lives, and, in many cases, through the pasts of ancestors who have affected us, and it connects these threads into patterns that help us understand our personal identities in ways that make sense for our present selves and our future prospects.

A vital personal identity requires a balance between what we already know about ourselves—our past actions, our present characteristics, our ancestral roots—and our aspirations for the future. We are best able to make sense of our lives when we integrate a look at where we've been with a look at where we wish to go. An ancient proverb has it, "Unless you know the road you have come down, you cannot know where you are going."

Identity formation is a lifelong project that begins in adolescence and continues to be a foundational psychological undertaking for all of adulthood. The initial structure of a personal identity is erected during the adolescent years. Around the time of puberty, rapid neural growth makes possible two intellectual capacities necessary for building a stable personal identity: (1) the ability to combine our disparate acts and features into generalized traits that make an overall statement about what we are like and (2) the ability to envision the future in a systematic way that has implications for our present choices. When these developing capacities are brought to bear on our intimations of who we are and where we are heading, our personal identities are hatched.

Many features of our personal identities are "sticky," continuing over years of our lives. One example might be the place where we grew up. There's a line from an old song that goes, "You can take the boy out of New York, but you can't take New York out of the boy." People who move away from their childhood homes from just about everywhere can feel this way: they keep identifying as Greeks, Aussies, Southerners, islanders, urbanites, country folk, and so on. They retain a longing for "home" and a keen sense of belonging to their birthplaces even if they never revisit them.

Other sticky features of identity include religious upbringing, social class, physical features, and temperamental dispositions. If you were raised Christian, you might never go to church as an adult or consider yourself among the faithful, yet that religious category with its particular emotional tenor may still cling to your identity. If you grew up in a working-class neighborhood, you may retain a blue-collar identification even after you've earned an advanced degree and pursued a professional vocation. If you were a severely underweight child, a sense of fragility may linger even after you've grown up, gained weight, and chalked up a list of sports successes.

Yet despite their constant features, our personal identities evolve over time; they are not fossilized at any point along the way. The formation and re-formation of identity is a lifelong project. The longer we live, the more material we have to rework in the particular personal identities that have carried us through the many decisions and endeavors of our lives to date.

How do we go about doing this? Sometimes we redefine ourselves in response to other people's reactions to our behavior. They may tell us we are graceful or clumsy, generous or stingy, good-humored or cranky, and such comments may affect how we think about ourselves. Sometimes we redefine ourselves on our own as we observe our own behavior. We may take a more objective look at our achievements and decide to shed an old sense of ourselves as, say, lazy or ineffective. We may decide that we're brave after voicing an unpopular opinion at a town hall meeting.

In an effort at systematic self-reflection such as a life review, we can intentionally work on revisiting our identities. When we do this, we play an active role in inventing our own futures: we determine the kinds of people we will become. In the case of my own life review, I was able to connect my experience of growing up without a father to a bundle of positive and negative dispositions, ranging from self-reliance to wariness. I figured out that my mother's secrecy about my father's whereabouts set limits on my family life and stunted my ability to appreciate and connect with an extended circle of relatives. As this new awareness expanded my social outlook, I was able to improve that dimension of my personal functioning by actively reaching out and making even distant family members know how much I valued them. Perhaps most revealingly, as I describe at the close of this chapter, I learned why my schooling took the unlikely course it did, transforming everything that was to come for me after that.

My understanding of who I am and how I got here became clearer to me, more grounded in the actual realities of my past. This led to modifications to my present identity that helped me deal with challenges such as resolving resentments and regrets, affirming the life I've had so far, and charting a purposeful way forward.

Finding and Pursuing Purpose

There is one key capacity that is not strictly necessary for personal identity but provides a big boost to the strength and sturdiness of an identity when available. It is not an intellectual capacity (though the mind plays a role in it); rather, it is a motivating force that develops into a character strength. This capacity is *purpose*. Among all the pillars of personal identity, purpose—when present—is the most robust. The threads most likely to provide continuity and stability over our past, present, and future lives are the purposes that we have dedicated ourselves to over the years and decades.

Finding purpose paves the way to a vigorous and fulfilling personal identity. In turn, a vigorous personal identity promotes the pursuit of sustaining purposes. Identity and purpose go hand in hand over the course of development, bolstering each other in a symbiotic way. Capturing the dynamic interplay between our purposes and our personal identities as they evolve together over the years is a primary focus of a life review.

As a life-span developmental psychologist, I've become interested in how purpose develops and contributes to identity at all phases of life. My research on this topic began twenty years ago with a study of purpose among adolescents who were just beginning their journeys toward the creation of purposeful identities. Since then, I have followed people's search for purpose into the later years of life, with studies of subjects as old as ages fifty to ninety. In every age period that I have observed, purpose stands out as a key to positive personal identity.

Purpose has long been identified in philosophy and theology as an essential component of a well-directed life. In recent years, support for this long-standing intuition has come from studies in psychological science and medicine that have documented important benefits associated with purpose. Such benefits can include energy and motivation, resilience under pressure, emotional stability, academic and vocational achievement, trust in the affirmative value of life, and a sense of direction that can withstand episodic periods of uncertainty and confusion. Recent writings in medicine, especially in gerontology, have posited that purpose contributes to health throughout the life span. In response, educational organizations worldwide are dedicating themselves to the task of helping people find and sustain purpose in their lives. The features of purpose that spur motivation and achievement also have the potential to improve the human condition. Purposeful people contribute to beneficial causes of all kinds.

Insightful writings about purpose predate my research. Austrian psychiatrist Victor Frankl, while imprisoned in a German concentration camp, conceived a psychological theory that identifies purpose as a noble antidote to life's destabilizing misfortunes and stresses. Frankl wrote that commitment to a purpose can provide resilience against psychological maladies such as anxiety, depression, and despair. In a positive sense, purpose can provide inspiration, energy, and contentment. Although his theory was published in English as Man's Search for Meaning, Frankl in fact used the German word Zweck, connoting "purpose" rather than "meaning."

Frankl founded a school of psychological counseling called "logotherapy," based on the idea that purpose should serve as a primary objective of a well-lived human life—not last in line after the satisfaction of a host of biological and material desires, as other schools of psychology (such as behaviorism and Freudianism) had claimed. Frankl's ideas about purpose were nonreligious: he emphasized purposeful engagements of a secular-humanistic variety. More recently, Pastor Rick Warren offered an influential examination of faith-based, Christian purposes in his best-selling *The Purpose-Driven Life*. Although distinct in their focuses, Frankl's and Warren's writings both are rich in insights about the psychological benefits of purpose.

My own focus has been on the entire range of purposes, from the mundane to the heroic, that provide direction, meaning, and fulfillment to people of all ages, abilities, and backgrounds. I have looked for purposes wherever I can find them, and I've tried to explain how they develop and how they affect those who pursue them. Since beginning my own life review, I've become increasingly intrigued by how purpose can be revealed in retrospect, and how a backward glance at our purposeful trajectories can propel us forward in new ways.

What, exactly, is purpose? Before my team and I began our research into how purpose develops, we examined how the term had been used in earlier writings within fields such as philosophy, theology, and the social sciences. Naturally we found inconsistencies—that's the way of language, even in scholarly fields. But we found enough consensus to derive a definition that captures the key features of this uniquely powerful psychological capacity. Our definition, now used widely in the field of human development, is as follows:

Purpose is an active commitment to accomplish aims that are both meaningful to the self and of consequence to the world beyond the self.

Although purpose is associated with related concepts such as passion and meaning (and is often spoken of interchangeably with such concepts), it has its own unique definition. This is important to understand, because science doesn't need more than one term for the same concept, nor should it use the same term differently on separate occasions. When a doctor writes you a prescription, it is essential that the meaning of the term the doctor uses is identical to the meaning of the term the pharmacist uses, or you may end up with the wrong medicine. It is equally essential to have one and only one term for each body part and to keep these terms distinct from one another. If the terms "kidney" and "spleen" were used interchangeably, abdominal surgery would be a harrowing experience.

Purpose can be found everywhere that people strive to accomplish something worthwhile. It can be found in a parent caring for a child. It can be found in workers doing their jobs with pride and a sense of social responsibility. A citizen who shows up to vote, or to campaign for a favorite candidate, displays civic purpose. A neighbor organizing a block party shows community purpose. Members of religious congregations are pursuing purposes of faith or spirituality. Musicians practicing scales, artists painting the colors of a sunset, and poets crafting poems are pursuing aesthetic purposes. Supervisors who train employees for the sake of their vocational growth are manifesting mentoring purposes.

Purpose is a relatively late-developing capacity. Studies from our lab and elsewhere have found that only about one in five adolescents between the ages of twelve and twenty-two have a fully developed sense of purpose. It is rare for children younger than twelve to exhibit full purpose. Many young people do not find sustaining purposes until the end of their twenties. Some do not become purposeful until mid-adulthood. This late development is unusual in human life: most important psychological capacities grow rapidly during the child and adolescent years.

Studies have revealed a common pattern among young people who do find purpose. The first step is the child's discovery of interests and talents that are compelling. Peter Benson, a founder of the "positive youth development" approach, called such interests and talents "sparks" and asserted convincingly that every child has his or her own particular sparks. People who eventually turn their sparks into purposes discover two revelations as they learn more about the world: (1) something in the world needs to be improved, corrected, or added to; (2) I myself have the ability to make a contribution to this.

The task of pursuing certain purposes—such as heroic challenges such as curing cancer or alleviating poverty—may be daunting. Or it may be quite ordinary, as in those who dedicate themselves to raising a family, to conventional vocations, or to any number of everyday purposes that contribute to the functioning of human society. Purposes need not be heroic or extraordinary to provide psychological and social benefits. In the course of a life review, we may realize that certain activities and choices that we took for granted at the time we engaged in them were in fact driven by a purposeful aim, providing us with the satisfaction that purpose conveys.

It was during high school that I acquired my interest in research and writing, envisioning a possible career as a journalist or scientist. This became my first real career purpose. Before that, my childhood imagination had me employed as a deep-sea fisherman (going after whales!), a baseball player, a military commander, and so on down a long list of youthful male fantasies. But once I had some experience with research and writing, my boyhood fantasies were replaced by a future vision that was exciting enough, and far more likely. The prospect of conducting research to find something new and then informing the world about it struck me as a fascinating, worthwhile, and consequential vocation. It has taken different forms over the course of my life, but as I look back, I can see clearly the "dots" that connect them all.

I did not come upon the idea of doing research from any school courses I took. When I first entered high school, coursework was the furthest thing from my mind. I had grown up in a down-at-the-heels factory town that emanated a distinctly anti-intellectual ethos, and academic learning had little appeal for me. But then I had an experience during ninth grade that forever changed my attitude toward academic pursuits.

I had joined my high-school newspaper in order to cover sports. As a freshman, I was too young to make any of the school teams, but I enjoyed watching the games and hanging out with the older players. A rookie reporter with poor writing skills, I was assigned to cover games of absolutely no interest to anyone. One of those games was a practice match for our junior varsity against a group of Hungarian immigrant teenagers who had formed a soccer team. Soccer was not a major school sport in the United States back then, and junior varsity soccer was of low status at our school. But the game turned out to be an interesting spectacle, with the young Hungarian players demonstrating amazing skills that they had acquired in Europe.

But that was not the story that captured my attention. I stayed around after the game to speak with the immigrant players. They clearly had very little in a material sense. Their mothers had packed them sandwiches of bacon fat and green peppers, and I remember feeling sorry for the boys who had only these for lunch. Yet the boys were full of spirit, and they were having a blast in their new country. They spoke excitedly about coming to America, about the hard lives they'd left behind, about what political freedom meant to their families, and about their hopes for prosperous futures. All this opened a world of cultural and historical knowledge to me that went far beyond what I had ever heard about.

When my story appeared in the newspaper, my friends read it and commented that they found it fascinating. Subsequently, as I had more newspaper writing experiences of this kind, I had little trouble devoting myself to classroom writing assignments. I was determined to learn the skills I needed to pursue the new purpose I had discovered. My choice of a career as a researcher can be traced back to the real satisfaction I discovered while reporting for my school newspaper.

In our time, most of us are called upon to construct our own individual purposes out of our inclinations, talents, and convictions. This is both a privilege and a challenge that past generations rarely had, since their life directions were more likely to be defined by ready-made commitments provided by society, religion, or vocations assigned to them when they were young. The task of choosing a vocational commitment for oneself does not come easy. No doubt it's the reason why, in our studies, we find young people who are drifting with little or no direction. Some of them are searching without success for meaningful commitments. Some are not even searching or have quit trying. It's those who never began searching, or who have given up entirely, who find it hardest to acquire purpose and experience its many benefits.

There are other points of resistance particular to our own confusing epoch. Unlike previous generations, we share little sense of national purpose. The idea that there might be collective ideals or principles that we could join together and dedicate ourselves to seems almost antiquated in our cynical age. As I learned about my father's life journey and compared it to my own, I took note that he grew up in a time that swept an entire generation of men into World War II. Reading over the documents that tell the story of my father's transition from schoolboy to soldier, it is clear to me that, like many in his time, my father found purpose only when he was called to military service. Other ready-made purposes that people could easily slip into also have receded. Belief systems and institutions of all kinds—civic, academic, religious, and cultural—have come under attack, or have fallen into disrepute, or have faded away from lack of interest among today's populace. As a consequence, purpose is not even on the radar screen of many people now.

This presents a puzzling problem: How can someone not looking for a purpose acquire one? When I had a chance to address one question to a man wiser than me, this was the one I chose to ask. The occasion was the opening of the Dalai Lama's North American Center in Vancouver, and I was one of a half dozen scholars who had been invited to engage in a public "dialogue" with His Holiness. After each presentation, the speaker was allowed to ask one question. Mine was, How can you help someone find purpose if they are not looking for it? The Dalai Lama's answer, which I only vaguely grasped at the time, was that you should reveal to the person *both* the barrenness of a life without purpose *and* the positive rewards of a life with purpose. You need to do *both*, he emphasized, and do it in as dramatic a way as possible. One point without the other would prove insufficient. To put it in a way that no doubt does injustice to the depth of the master's wisdom, this is a stick-and-carrot approach.

My autobiographical self-examination helped me comprehend this message in a more concrete way. I recalled my initial discovery of my attraction to research and writing while working for my high-school newspaper: I recognized this as a "carrot" that drew me forward. Around the same time, I also had a whack from a "stick." I was shaken out of my lethargic approach to schoolwork by harsh feedback from a teacher who cared enough to pay attention to my poor attitude when I started high school. This occurred when I turned in a weekly assignment and made the ill-advised comment "I hope this paper doesn't matter much." The teacher—an older gentleman who was stern but caring—sat me down and glared at me for what seemed an eternity. Finally he barked, "Mr. Damon! I want you to always remember that *everything* you do in this world matters!" This remark conveyed the demands of purpose, and I have always remembered it. Interestingly, another stick came from the Dalai Lama himself. During the dialogue, he also had the opportunity to ask each speaker one question. His Holiness turned to me with a fierce look and asked me what I was now going to do *in action* to implement the nice ideas in my talk. I admit to coming up a bit blank on this at the time. After lots of reflection, I jolted myself into more direct efforts to communicate findings from my research on human development to broader public audiences, and to promote community relationships that could provide new occasions for people of all ages to experience purposeful activities.

After adolescence, the adult years are marked by initial commitments to purposes that can endure for a lifetime: building a family, choosing a vocation, serving God, advancing a cherished cause, becoming an engaged citizen. Commitments to purposes in early adulthood are marked by ambition, high hopes, and idealism. The mid-adulthood years see realistic recognitions of what's survived from those early hopes and dreams. Purposes that have produced results tend to endure, and those become the purposes that define our identity. We begin to look back to see what's worked, and we adjust present and future expectations accordingly, adapting to the realities of success and failure that events have brought.

Later adulthood offers opportunities to find new purposes that build on, or replace, ones that have energized our earlier lives. Some earlier purposes become obsolete because of changes in circumstances due to age. Retirement is a primary example of this. No matter how dedicated a doctor has been to the purpose of healing the sick, once the doctor retires, that purpose can no longer be pursued in the same manner. On the family front, once children have grown and started homes of their own, the purpose of parenting takes on a new and more limited meaning. Parents still retain the purpose of seeing that their offspring are doing well but do not need to monitor their children's daily activities with the same intensity as when they had to watch and make sure their children were safely crossing the street.

As people fulfill or outgrow their early purposes, they can seek new ones. They have additional time, and the same need, to accomplish things of consequence in the world. Because of this opportunity to pursue further purposes as earlier ones wind down, aging expert Marc Freedman calls the later years of life the "encore" period.

Our Stanford research team studied a representative sample of 1,200 women and men aged fifty to ninety-two and found large numbers of fully purposeful individuals. Encouragingly, we found the prevalence of full purpose to be higher in adulthood—especially late adulthood—than in youth. Overall, the prevalence of purpose was significantly higher in people over sixty-five than among middle-aged adults, who in turn demonstrated more purpose than young adults and adolescents. This means that there is growth throughout the life span in this essential capacity.

Our finding that many older adults are purpose-driven contributors to the world discredits widespread stereotypes of elderly people as withdrawn from key life roles, burdens on society, or focused only on leisure. They're not just sitting at home dozing or out sunbathing. In our research, we've observed numerous people in late adulthood who, after retiring from their jobs, establish "encore careers" such as tutoring or home health care, that fill their lives with new purposes.

As with younger people, we found that older people with high levels of purpose enjoyed benefits of adaptation such as energy, resilience, and an interest in learning new skills. Purposes that motivate older people vary as widely as the human condition itself. Some pursue new family purposes, such as caring for grandchildren. Some volunteer for work in their local communities. Some pursue charitable aims, such as fund-raising for nonprofits dedicated to alleviating poverty. Some pursue aesthetic purposes, such as painting, storytelling, or musical performances. Some become dedicated to animal rescue or to their own pets. Some become increasingly swept up by religious faith and other spiritual involvements. Our study also revealed that purpose among older people is not affected by health or economic condition. Purpose is widely available to people from all backgrounds, all socioeconomic statuses, and all ethnicities and genders; even poor health does not preclude purposeful pursuits.

The search for purpose never ceases. As we age, we entertain new aspirations and take on new commitments. In doing this, we draw on interests and capacities we developed earlier in life. In this way, the accomplishments of our early years can set the stage for a later life of meaning, fulfillment, and contributions to the common good. A life review can bring all of this into focus, accelerating the discovery of our "encore" purposes and affording new satisfaction as we look back at the driving forces of our earlier lives.

Purpose is a lifelong need, as relevant as we age as when we are young. We may imagine it will be a straight line when we look forward as young people. But when we look back, we see it as more evolving, more meandering, and less predictable: our purposes change as we adapt to our changing circumstances and those of the world at large. A life review offers us a way to look back and connect the dots, starting with our first glimmers of purpose in adolescence. It can help us recall the purposes we've had in our lives, integrate them with our present circumstances, and envision opportunities for further purposeful work.

Looking Back at My Meandering and Unpredictable Road

High school was the setting for my discovery of purpose, as I noted earlier in this chapter. In ninth grade, to borrow from my interpretation of the Dalai Lama's insights, I had both a stick and a carrot experience: the stick was the harsh admonition I received from my stern but caring teacher; the carrot was the thrill I found in writing for my school newspaper.

What I did not mention in that account was the unusual school context I was operating in, or how I got there. I knew all along that the school I attended was unusual. But how I got there was a revelation only recently uncovered by my family discovery search—one that radically changed my view of how the foundations of my personal identity came to be. As I noted in chapter 1, in my first visit with Aunt Verna, she stunned me with the information that I had attended the same school as my father, something I had never before known.

The school was Phillips Academy Andover, which is widely known as one of the world's top-quality boarding schools. But Andover was not widely known in the circles that I grew up in. Among my friends and relatives in down-at-the-heels Brockton, no one had ever heard of the place. Once when I came home from Andover on school vacation, I found out that my friends thought I had been sent away to a military school called "Hanover" because I had gotten myself in trouble of some kind. This was the state of their knowledge about it. My family's economic state hovered somewhere around lower middle class. The likelihood that a boy from Brockton with my social background would attend—or even know about—an elite prep school such as Andover bordered on nil.

So how did I make the journey to this fabled educational institution, forty geographical miles but a social-cultural world apart from my home turf? The simple answer is—my mother. Behind that answer is the complex, shadowy figure of my father. It is clear to me now that my mother urged me to go there, and arranged the necessary scholarship, because she knew that my father had been a student there. At least in this one way she must have been trying to re-create my father in me.

Brief and broken though my mother's marriage was, the man she married must have seemed admirable enough to her that she guided her only son in his direction. I had no inkling of this until my visit with

Aunt Verna. Unaware that my father had preceded me at Andover by twenty-two years, and pretty much oblivious on all counts, I was following in my father's footsteps.

My time at Andover transformed my future. It provided me with opportunities to pursue purposes that I could fully commit to, purposes I may not have found had I been on a different educational path. Ultimately, the purposes I found shaped the identity I have developed over the course of my life. Although I myself chose the purposes I eventually pursued, I was guided onto the educational path that led me to those purposes. My attendance at Andover was an occurrence beyond my reckoning or control, something that "happened" to me without my awareness of why it happened.

Not everything about who we are is self-determined. We develop our identities within certain frameworks we are given. Yet we still may play an active role in one way or another. My life review and the explorations it prompted would reveal to me that my father's time at Andover was quite different from mine, less earnest and less purposeful. His experience was shaped by his own aspirations, yearnings, and character, as was mine. The school affected his future, but in different ways than it affected mine. Wherever we have been placed on the road to identity, that road eventually leads through purpose, and on that part of our journeys, we propel ourselves.

4

Examining Early Character

UP THE FLIGHTS of stairs I ventured at 4:00 p.m. on a Friday, during a week when school was not in session. There were no signs of anyone else around. The once-familiar library, with its wooden shelves and smell of musty leather, receded beneath me as I climbed. On the top floor, I found a corridor so silent that I wondered whether anyone had been there in decades. At the end of the hushed hallway was an office with a closed, opaque-glass door. I tried the handle, not expecting the door to open. But it did! And there, alone in the room, sat a woman with a smile that seemed to say, "How nice to see someone coming to visit our cherished archival records!" Starting at the improbable time of 4:00 p.m. on a late-summer Friday, the magnificent lady records-keeper helped me dig into my father's schoolboy past.

It had stunned me to discover that my father went to the same school—Phillips Academy Andover—that I attended twenty-two years after him. In my quest to discover everything I could about my father and myself, I now realized that a key part of the story I was seeking lay buried in the school settings that united the two of us. What was his time there like? How did he do? What did his record there reveal about his early character?

And what about my own time there? I remembered those days only in vaguely nostalgic and imprecise ways, in keeping with the typical nature of memory. How did my schooling there compare with my father's experience? What's more, I had the same questions, for both my father and myself, about how we spent our college years. Once again, I had ended up in the same place as my father, Harvard, although that was a fact that I had always known, so it did not contain the mystery aura of the Andover revelation.

I arranged my trip to the Andover archives to coincide with one of my school reunions. A reunion is a time-traveling kind of trip on its own. This one felt like a temporal voyage across two generations. Thickening the air was the antique New England setting I was revisiting. It felt more like "Olde" than "New" England, a scene straight out of Dickens. Nowhere did this feel more the case than the timeworn place where the school kept its former students' records, on the top floor of its venerable Oliver Wendell Holmes Library.

My investigation into the school and college experiences of my father and me proved to be one of the high points of my discovery quest. It was truly amazing to view long-ago teacher reports about us, to gaze upon original letters written about my father by my grandmother and grandfather or about me by my mother, to compare and contrast the school climates that shaped the two of us during our high school years, and to reflect on our respective characters in light of what the records showed. I would leave Andover that weekend feeling like I was beginning to know my father, and myself, a lot better.

There are many things that we can know about people: where they live, what they look like, what kind of job they have, what kinds of food or music they like, how much money they have, and so on. But only when we acquire a sense of a person's *character* do we know who he or she really is. The term derives from an ancient Greek word meaning "a distinctive mark or stamp" (such as a sharp engraving). This indicates that character goes deep. A perfectly good definition of character, in keeping with the term's etymological root, can be found online: "The mental and moral qualities distinctive to an individual."

A word that has been used in modern-day psychological writings to cover much the same ground as character is the term "personality." Although the two terms share the common objective of describing an individual's behavioral traits, there are sharp differences in focus between them. "Personality" refers to any kind of consistent behavioral pattern that we may expect to see in a particular individual, whereas character refers to patterns that support or deter morally virtuous behavior. So, for example, it's common to speak of "neurotic" personalities, "fun-loving" ones, "odd" ones, and so on, but such adjectives would rarely be used to describe a person's character. Conversely, adjectives such as "honest," "fair-minded," "compassionate," and "responsible"—or, in reverse, "dishonest," "selfish," "irresponsible"—are more likely used as indicators of character than as descriptors of personality.

Character connotes behavioral habits acquired over the course of development. When these habits are virtuous, they provide social strengths for the individual and pro-social benefits for society. This is the reason why "positive psychologists" and educators have found value in this ancient term, and why I use it here for examining the distinctive qualities demonstrated by my father and me during our respective school years.

The formation of character begins early in life. It starts with the habits of heart and mind that children acquire in families, friendships, religious practices, and other lived exposures to the world. Children learn these habits—called "virtues" when they are positive in nature—through instruction, observation, and reflections on the outcomes of their own actions.

During childhood and adolescence, school is one of the major settings for acquiring and testing habits of character. Children spend about a third of their waking time in school, and they conduct relationships with teachers and peers that can have lasting influences on their behavior. Schooling highlights character virtues such as responsibility, future-mindedness, honesty, and diligence. Although not every child learns such virtues in school, most children at least become aware that such virtues are called for in life due to both direct and indirect messages from their teachers and schoolmates.

Schooling does not operate alone in conveying virtues to young people. One principle of psychological development is that children learn best by receiving clear and consistent messages in numerous ways and multiple contexts. When young people hear similar messages from all the people in their lives, they take the messages to heart. Students learn honesty in a deep and lasting way if their teachers explain why cheating undermines the academic mission, their parents talk with them about the importance of telling the truth, their sports coaches discourage deceit in play because it defeats the purpose of fair competition, and their friends indicate why lies destroy the trust needed for close relationships. If all this happens, students acquire a lived sense of honesty and an understanding of why it's important for every human relationship they will participate in, now and in the future.

In many cases, children who do not demonstrate character virtues during their school years go on to acquire them later in life. Contrary to outdated psychological theories claiming that character is fixed at an early age, the possibility of character growth never ceases as long as we remain alive. People learn from their experiences, and especially from their mistakes. Many students who were reprimanded for errant behavior in school eventually learn to do better, often because of the reprimands. Also, life itself offers new opportunities for acquiring character strengths long after the school years have passed. Knowing what a person was like in school cannot tell you how the person's whole life story will turn out.

Still, early habits leave a trace, even after they have been mostly outgrown. A child who habitually withdraws from peers can learn to become less shy (even gregarious, as studies have found), yet rumblings of the child's early shyness may reemerge from time to time. We all are complex. We all "contain multitudes," as the poet Walt Whitman wrote about himself. The character of any person is a unique mix of traits reflecting that person's special life experiences and personal choices. Some traits reflect long-standing behavioral patterns and others reflect new or changed ways of acting. To know a person well—including ourselves—it's necessary to know as much of the person's life story as possible, from beginning to end. It is essential to appreciate the full complexities of character a person has developed over time if we are to understand the entire range of that person's behavior.

An Archival Journey Back in Time

The helpful records-keeper plucked from the shelves a worn book from the 1950s listing alumni who had died by then. There, buried among thousands of names of Andover deceased, she found one "Sgt Philip Damon." Well, I mentally sighed, at least I wasn't the only person who believed that my father died in the war. From that book, the lady extracted some identifying code that led her, now sparkling with the thrill of the chase, to take me through a door behind her desk into a room with about the same degree of freshness as King Tut's tomb when it was opened. Before me stood a row of antiquated steel file cabinets of the kind that appear in offices shown in 1940s *film noir* detective movies. In a cabinet that had been coded by some diligent records-keeper preceding my own devoted guide dwelled a thick cardboard storage file with my father's name on it.

Back in the main office, I opened the folder slowly, and time stopped. There were letters to the school from his parents (my grandmother and grandfather), still vivid with exclamations of parental concern. There were report cards, test scores, and lengthy treatises from counselors and teachers about his behavior, his character, his talents, and his attitudes— the latter not so good. It turns out that my father was a slacker. He lasted three years at the school before being dismissed for lack of effort

Verna, Grandmother Damon, and my father before high school

and desultory approach to schoolwork. During those three years he gave his teachers abundant chances to record indicators of his boyhood character. In that folder, in full detail, were lavish accounts of my father's adolescent behavior, colored by the biases and attitudes of those days.

As an educator and developmental psychologist, I'm familiar with the sorts of things that teachers nowadays comment on in a student's file. High on contemporary lists are notes about a student's stress levels, self-esteem (or lack of it), interests, and, for an incredibly large number of students, special learning disabilities (chronic fatigue, dyslexia, and ADHD are common ones). Today, teacher reports tend to be sympathetic, child-centered, and almost clinical in their efforts to diagnose learning problems that many students are seen to be suffering from. In comparison, my father's files were full of admonitions and pejorative terms such as "slacker" and "shirker." Much like the underperforming students of today, he too had learning problems. But rather than conveying sympathy or child-centered concern, his files smacked of disapproval for his behavior. He was not living up to the school's standards, and his teachers held little doubt that it was his own behavioral choices that were responsible for his disappointing performance. Their emphasis was on my father's work habits and his character, rather than on any clinical condition that might have been beyond his control. His teachers pressed him to do more. None of them seemed worried about his level of stress.

Nonetheless, my father's teachers did care enough to write lengthy, concerned statements about his deficiencies, accompanied by insistent recommendations about how he should improve. The files were thickly descriptive, a treasure trove for an investigator with my agenda. They were austere in tone but lavish in content. They told me a lot about the culture of education at that time, and they told me even more about my father, my special new interest.

Later that year, I continued my archival quest at Andover by retrieving my own school records there. Then I extended the quest to my father's records at Harvard, where he had been a freshman and a sophomore before joining the army after the start of World War II. My father's college records were less evocative than his Andover ones, but they contained further grist for my discovery mill and at least one intriguing gem. Finally, to complete my archival searches, I sent for my Harvard records, which again were less revealing than the Andover files but still helpful in filling in my memory gaps regarding my college years. Supplied with these thick troves of information, I was prepared to examine the way the two of us went about the task of developing character in school and college.

Early Signs of Character

Every school envelops its students in some sort of moral climate. The choices a school makes about what sort of moral climate to establish can leave lasting marks on students. At its founding in 1778, Phillips

Academy Andover proclaimed its mission to be the cultivation of academic excellence and character (today's language has it as "knowledge and goodness"). The school's traditional motto is "Non Sibi" (*not for self*); and that was the ethic that defined its approach to character education both in my day and my father's. "Non Sibi" is a source of ethical continuity that links the early training of generations of Andover students in other-oriented habits of character.

Yet, despite continuities of this sort, character education also evolves in other ways over time. A school's efforts to promote character often reflect the values of its day in how it guides and evaluates its students. This was as true at Andover as at any other school. The school that my father attended remained in some ways identical to the school I attended, but there were differences that reflected changes in American society over the years separating our school days.

Most noticeable was a sterner tone in my father's day, accompanied by stricter codes of enforcement. Although the conduct expected of students had not changed in any noticeable way, the manner in which the school enforced those behaviors had markedly relaxed by my time there.

In a recent book about the Bush family political dynasty, I found a compelling account of Andover's changes from my father's time there to my own. It turns out that the elder President Bush (George Herbert Walker) was one class ahead of my father there, and I was one class ahead of his son, George W. Here's what the book says about the Andover of my father's (and the elder George Bush's) era, the mid-to-late 1930s:

> The school was committed to developing the "whole man." Academics were certainly important. But discipline and character were more so, with strict rules on dress, table manners, and an academic code of conduct. Claude Fuess [the headmaster] . . . would walk around campus, his starched white collar like a tall, white picket fence around his neck, barking out orders to students and faculty alike.

In my (and George W.'s) time at Andover—the early-to-mid 1960s—there were still strict rules on dress, manners, and an academic code of conduct. We were required to attend chapel every morning at 7:00 a.m., dressed in coats and ties, before breakfast, without regard to whatever the wintry New England weather might throw at us as we groggily stumbled across campus. But there were no teachers or housemasters walking around barking orders at us. Our relations with adults on campus were cordial and informal. As for student attitudes, the book on the Bushes accurately describes the tone of our 1960s cohort this way: "a pervasive sense of sarcasm has descended on the campus."

In an account that provoked even more sarcasm among Andover students at the time, a *Life* magazine reporter wrote a piece about "negativism" he observed while visiting our campus. Responding to this piece, the school's administration explained that this was just a sign that we were more "individualistic" than earlier cohorts. This led one school leader to worry that we may have been lacking what he called "group guts." The '60s definitely had arrived at Andover.

There was another crucial difference between my father's attendance at Andover and my own. Not only had the school evolved, but my father and I went there under very different social and economic circumstances. My father grew up in an old New England WASP family that sent its children to elite prep schools as a matter of course. My upbringing, wholly disconnected from my father's family, was a world apart. I was raised by a single mother with modest help from her extended family of recent immigrants. I went to public schools through ninth grade. I had every expectation of going to Brockton High, where I hoped to attain a record sufficient enough to win a scholarship to any college that would take me. Only after my recent life-review search do I now know that my mother, unbeknownst to me, arranged for me to follow in my father's educational footsteps.

As my father's school records would reveal, the two of us did not proceed down our school paths in anything like the same way. Unlike my father, I experienced Andover as a tough environment, socially as well as academically. I struggled to fit in. Academically, I worked hard, and not always successfully, at least at first. For an agonizingly long time, I barely kept my head above water. But with persistence, I eventually got on top of things and found my strengths and interests; in the end, I accomplished enough to gain admission to Harvard, a competitive slog even back then. My father, in contrast, enjoyed his Andover life at the start. He had what we'd nowadays call "too much fun." He breezed by with little or no effort for three years, until he used up all his chances. Then, with not much to his credit, he flunked out.

But my father's failure at Andover could not have been predicted. Until his high-school years, he showed plenty of potential. His records contain a reference letter for him sent by his previous school, a small private academy in western Massachusetts. It was a boarding school for seventh- and eighth-grade youngsters, and his entire class consisted of only four students. Every student there must have received a wealth of attention. The school's letter for him described his character and intelligence in generally glowing terms, with just a hint of apprehension about his work habits ('works best under pressure") and rebellious nature ("tiresomely argumentative").

> Philip Damon is thoroughly honorable and above-board. There is no doubt that his ability is outstanding. . . . He learns quickly, reasons well, and he has an unusual fund of general information, but is not especially original or imaginative. As for industry, like many boys he works best under pressure, but we are confident that he will respond to the stimulus of keener competition in a larger school. . . . His chief fault at the moment is his tendency to be tiresomely argumentative, but as he is fundamentally a fair-minded and well-balanced boy, we are sure this is a passing phase.

Once at Andover, though, it did not take long for my father to undercut these mostly favorable expectations. His ninth-grade counselor's report noted that "he worked only moderately, and did not achieve what he should have. He cannot 'take it' well under pressure in class." The counselor attributed this shortcoming to overindulgence on the part of my grandmother: "Mother and boy inclined to be a bit 'soft' in relationship—boy rather soft."

Still, this ninth-grade counselor approved of my father's personal qualities: "Character good . . . well-liked, rather attractive in his 'big-puppy' way . . . very nice boy . . . pleasant attitude towards people and things." The counselor also used a descriptor that has me scratching my head in bafflement and, I suppose, amusement. My father, according to the report, was "quite a dick" (I'm sure the counselor was not using this term in the way it's meant today!). Indeed, my father's following-year report notes that he was a "very capable dicker," drawing on the same root term. Despite much research, I have been unable to pin down the 1930s meaning of "a capable dicker." I'm guessing that it meant a charming rascal of some sort. Language, too, evolves.

When I opened my father's second-year guidance report, I was taken aback to see a name, and hear a voice, I recognized. The relatively short interval between my father's time at Andover and my own meant that some of the teachers who had known my father were still around when I was a student. Indeed, my favorite English teacher, Hart Day Leavitt, wrote a vivid description of my father for his tenth-grade report. Mr. Leavitt, familiar to me as a kindly, eminently congenial teacher, summed up my father's performance in this sharply critical way:

> His sense of values is essentially sound [but] he has no strong ambition. Has a somewhat facile mind which, however, is far from organized. Not at all diligent. Achievement has been remarkably erratic. In general, he has come far from reaching his capabilities. Accomplishments have been very few; does not go into anything deeply enough.

Mr. Leavitt did credit my father with a "mature sense of humor." But this compliment was qualified by the following caveat: "The difficulty is that he smiles at his own failings and then does nothing about them." The upside was that he was easygoing, gregarious, fun to be with, and trustworthy. The downside was that he did not apply himself. His underachieving downside was summed up in a word: "loafer." As an irritated aside, Mr. Leavitt noted that "his room has been the sloppiest in the house all year."

Reading these words, I could hear the voice of my cherished English teacher in my head, echoing as it once had through our classroom, expounding on Shakespeare and Chaucer. Did he recall my father while observing me two decades later? Did he know we were father and son, and if so, what would he have thought about our similarities and differences? Sadly, I would learn that Mr. Leavitt died before I began my journey of discovery, so all I had were the words written in those brittle old files.

As my father's "loafing" got him deeper and deeper into trouble at Andover, his files swelled with failed courses, warnings, and periods of probation. Report after report rings with exasperation at my father's "poor attitude," his "low effort," and his persistent failure to apply himself. His teachers' exasperation was sharpened by their sense that he was a boy of "unusual ability." One wrote, "Whenever he chooses to do a good job, he could do it far better than the ordinary boy in this school." By the eleventh grade, he was considered a "problem case" who was a "poor influence" on his classmates.

His behavior became unruly: "Damon has frequented the hang-outs in town and has given the impression of not being seriously interested in his career at Andover." More than once it was written that he was "girl-crazy," dating numerous young ladies at any one time—not an easy thing to do while living at boarding school! He was also suspected of faking illnesses in order to get out of schoolwork.

On occasion the boy has reported himself as unwell when his doctor was unable to discover anything the matter with him. . . . He reports himself as having been very ill, obtains excuses from his classes on this ground, and suddenly becomes quite well as soon as the classes are over. . . . Reports have come to us that Damon has used artificial means of inducing illness (which we cannot or do not wish to attempt to prove), and indeed Mr. James found him reportedly with a fever lying in his bed in his pajamas with the window open.

There were financial consequences for my father's poor performances. During his years at Andover, he lost a total of $2,330 in tuition benefits that the school (in those days) awarded from its endowment to students of good standing. The value of this loss in today's dollars is $41,667. Although my father's parents were well-off, they were far from wealthy, and in their frugal New England lifestyle, this loss must have stung.

My father's repeated failings provoked letters from his parents beseeching the deans and headmaster for more help, leniency, and another chance. It's been heartbreaking for me to read my grandmother's and grandfather's agonized letters on their wayward son's behalf. Their anxious disappointment drips from every page. Intensifying the pain, my grandmother's letters make note of the initial stages of the then-undiagnosed disease (multiple sclerosis) that was to kill my grandfather by age fifty. My grandmother's distress lacked awareness of the deadly course that my grandfather's disease was to take, yet her apprehension showed, adding pathos to her letters.

Now, these many years later, I sympathize greatly with their parental pain. And I treasure the correspondence that expressed it. The letters from my grandparents that I retrieved from my father's Andover file are the only letters I have from them. Even though I was not their intended recipient, these letters mean a lot to me. They are the only vestiges of my paternal grandparents that I have. Beyond their personal value, the letters provide many clues about my grandparents' influences on my father's character development: my grandmother's loving over-indulgence; my grandfather's loving, ethical sternness. They also express their devotion toward their son, the boy who was to become my father less than a decade later.

My father finally was dismissed from Andover at the end of his third year, to the obvious dismay and frustration of his parents. For his senior year in high school, he was sent to a smaller, less demanding boarding school, where he compiled pretty much the same unsatisfactory record. Nonetheless, in the spring of 1941, he was admitted to the Harvard class of 1945. What criteria would have permitted the admission of a candidate such as my father is beyond me. Harvard had plenty of warning: highlighted in my father's college file is a reference letter from his senior year in school that had been submitted during the admissions procedure: "Due partly to laziness and partly to plain cussedness, he has never done the work of which he is capable . . . [he's] an excellent example of the kind of student who 'could if he would.' His failure to do outstanding work may be due to a certain immaturity, the result of spoiling by an overindulgent mother."

Was his admission to Harvard a by-product of the Great Depression's flattened economy, still very much in effect when my father applied to college? Or did admissions officers in those days take more generous views of a student's potential, with the hope that a student who seemed capable might turn out to be a late bloomer? Along with the many comments noting my father's laziness, his reference letters did contain statements such as "he is one of the brightest pupils I have ever taught, and if he can ever 'find himself' and apply himself to his work, I know he will make an excellent record." Perhaps the Harvard admissions office harbored hopes that my father would transform himself into a responsible student by the time he got to college.

If so, those hopes proved misguided. My father's performance did not change. He never "found himself" in college. He never applied himself to his work. There was the same academic underperformance, leading to academic probation by his sophomore year. Once again he was described as "girl-crazy," "party-mad," and "*wild.*" Of course, from my

EXAMINING EARLY CHARACTER | 83

vantage point, in regard to his relations with my mother, the girl-crazy part had a salubrious outcome: I'm very glad to be here.

My father's wildness now ratcheted itself up to the noisier, more public kind of mischief that older adolescents become capable of, and it got him in more serious trouble. A pointed letter by an angry dean describes one incident in colorful detail: a run-in, while drunk, with Cambridge policemen during a night of philandering in the tough part of town at a local dive, complete with an overnight stay in the city jail. Noteworthy on this occasion was that, rather than accepting the rebukes of the cops with discreet embarrassment, my father feistily protested their treatment of him and his fellow student marauders. His reaction foreshadowed a more consequential protest of authority that was to distinguish his army career and play a role in the reform of military justice in the US armed forces.

Interestingly, twenty-two years later, I also received a deserved dressing-down from a policeman in the same part of town after some friends and I were making too much noise one night (fortunately for me, there was no report to the college in our case). I've resisted making much of this particular comparison—after all, many college students act foolishly at some time or other. What I did find noteworthy in my reaction to reading about this incident in my father's files was how eager I was to compare myself to my father on any grounds I could find. In this and other ways, my quest to discover my father became a part of my quest to discover myself.

The bulk of what I learned about my father from his school and college reports did little to alter the impression I'd long harbored—that he was an irresponsible rogue. Yet hidden among the admonishments were signs that he had virtues to build on. He was in no way irredeemable (nor, in my view, is anyone). In his case, there is evidence throughout all his school records of notable honesty, friendliness, and compassion. He was always seen as a "nice boy" and "well-liked." His moral character—such as his trustworthiness—received frequent commendations. Even skeptical Mr. Leavitt wrote that "his sense of values is essentially sound."

As I would soon learn, in joining the army my father found the purpose that he lacked in his school and college days. Humans, especially
when they are young, do not stand still character-wise. Character is a
movie, not a snapshot. Life experience can change people for the better
or the worse. Even more importantly, people can change themselves.
Often they do so by dedicating themselves to larger purposes. In the
process, they gain insights about the kinds of people they wish to become,
and they strive to become those kinds of people.

In 1942, during the darkest moments of the century's gravest war,
my father volunteered for service in the US Army. Like many young
Americans of his generation, my father's student days came abruptly to
an end. He went into active duty in radio intelligence, serving in Europe
at the front. Pictures of him in his army uniform show him transformed
into a hardened soldier with a stern visage, no longer the soft, coddled
boy who played his way through school. He was only nineteen, but he
had the resolute face of a man on a mission. He appears to have developed what leading psychologist Angela Duckworth has compellingly
described as "grit."

No one can say what his motives for volunteering were. What mix
of patriotism, quest for adventure, avoidance of school drudgery, and/
or desire to make something of his life moved him to leave comfortable
New England for difficult and dangerous assignments in the heart of
war-torn Europe? As I discuss in chapter 5, the parts of my father's army
records that survive reveal a quality of character that was as admirable
as it was unexpected: moral courage.

Also surviving from my father's army years is a notation in New York
City's municipal records that now is of interest to me alone. The notation shows that my father married my mother on February 26, 1944.
Through some circumstance long buried in the trifles of history, my
father managed to return to the States from his European army station
and marry my mother. I was born in November of that year. By then,
my father was back in Europe for good, at least as far as my life was
concerned.

From Father to Son

My interest in my father's character development at every point turns my attention back to my own development. I also have a long-standing interest in character development: I have studied this from a scientific perspective for much of my career. My interests have been those of a developmental psychologist, exploring how people acquire the habits of heart and mind that, over time, turn into the virtues that constitute character. What are the roles of genetic dispositions, family influences, school, religion, and the social and historical contexts that we grow up in? Which experiences affect character, and how? Which people, ideas, and events influence our habits? What capacity do people have for fashioning their own characters through choices they can make?

The questions taken together suggest an initial answer to the question of how character develops. *All* the influences that the questions identify play some role. Which ones predominate, and how they combine to foster character growth, differ among individuals. But to examine the roots of anyone's character, we must consider parental influences, life experiences, peer and other social relations, inherited qualities, religious faith, and the active choices that the person has made to exert control over his or her destiny.

In my life, I had just one live-in parent, my mother, to guide my growth. Yet it turned out that my father, despite his complete absence, also exerted life-changing influence on me. He did so without knowing it, by revealing an extraordinary educational setting for my mother to put me in. It was deeply ironic, of course, that he himself had made such poor use of that stellar setting. But it was there, ready and waiting for me, a much less privileged but far more ambitious boy. Unlike my father, I took advantage of it.

In addition to parental influence, there are also genetic components to character—which may have a partial (though by no means complete) effect on one's behavior, at least early in life before other influences kick in. Did I inherit remnants of my father that might have been evident in *my* schoolboy behavior? As I searched through my own Andover and Harvard files looking for comparisons, this was one of the questions I had in mind.

My first-year school record at Andover, similar to that of my father's, reveals a mediocre student at best. In the words of my counselor, my performance "did not inspire." His comment does not surprise me. My memory of those early days at Andover is of feeling bewildered, adrift, and many times lost. I was not well prepared. What did surprise me was that my dorm master in my first year described me as "a very gay and ebullient fellow with a very pleasant and happy-go-lucky disposition." Not the way I remembered myself, but of special interest now that I've seen similar-sounding accounts of my father's disposition during his own early adolescence. Dispositions are prime candidates for heritability.

By my senior year, three years later, I had adapted well to school. In my file, there is a summary statement by the dean, written for college admissions purposes, that now captures my attention for a number of reasons. For one thing, it documents that I had become a serious and hardworking student: "Tall, slender, bespectacled, rather serious in aspect, a boy of distinctly better-than-average intelligence and performance." For another, it confirms that I had a quality that I did not remember having: gregariousness. (Strangely, though, the statement also included the descriptors "quiet and shy"; I recall the quiet and shy part better than the gregarious part.) It describes me as "generally a thoughtful and mature person." And it also conveys the density of misinformation that surrounded my father's whereabouts: it referred to me as "the only child of a widowed mother, father killed in World War II." The bubble of ignorance extended beyond me in those days.

A description from my dorm master during that final year offered a similar depiction with intriguing caveats. It noted that I was a "capable and intelligent boy who is earnestly concerned with his studies and . . . his aims go beyond [grades] and he is really interested in the material he studies and in ideas." His report noted my sociability, which pleased me when I first saw it: "In the dormitory Bill has shown himself to be a boy of very agreeable personality, always courteous and amiable, and one who has excellent relations with others who respect him highly. He enters the gatherings with enthusiasm, partakes in the discussion with keen interest, ideas, and a good moral sense."

As for the caveats:

Bill . . . likes nothing better than a good conversation, and if he finds one during study hours, he is happy to partake. This means late hours. . . . I think he would be better off if he were to regulate his time and put a little more order in his system.

He prides himself on being broad-minded and liberal, but he is apt to be stubborn and get no further than his own point of view which is often apt to be of the "off-beat" variety. I do have one criticism, which is of his housekeeping, which he does very badly. He cannot seem to bring himself to the point of keeping a semblance of neatness or order to his belongings.

Definitely certain shades of my father. I shared his gregarious and outgoing nature, some of his disorganized habits, and his streak of stubborn independence. I doubt there's a gene for sloppiness (and if there is, I outgrew it, as I've been told he did as well). But we did not outgrow our endemic stubborn streaks. My father showed independence by refusing to conform to school standards in an era when such standards were unquestioned and vigorously upheld; I expressed mine by taking school standards seriously in an era of rising skepticism about them. We were exercising our shared sense of independence in opposite ways. As for our gregariousness and outgoing social manners, psychological research suggests that inherited dispositions may play a role in such characteristics. When bolstered by my newly discovered realization that I've been an outgoing person from my school days, I now see my interpersonal manner as a continuing part of my identity.

Overall, it's clear to me that the Andover experience meant something very different to me than it did to my father. From the very beginning, as unprepared and lost as I felt, I treasured the chance to learn in such an intellectually stimulating setting. I knew from the start that I had a long way to go before I would become a mature, well-developed person, and I welcomed all the guidance and discipline from teachers who could help me get there. My father felt no such needs. He had grown up in a different world, amid circumstances that afforded him far more security and far more opportunity than I had ever sensed. What others readily had provided for him, I had to find for myself. My Andover education appeared to me as a miraculous, once-in-a-lifetime chance to achieve. This realization awakened in me a sense of purpose that my father had lacked during his own school years. The upside of deprivation is that it can give birth to ambition.

My Harvard files contained a surprise for me, and it was not something written. It was a photo of me when I was an entering student. In that picture, for the first time, I recognized in my facial image the features of my father that I discovered in a photo Aunt Verna sent me nine years ago (the first picture I had ever seen of my father). This recognition of our facial similarity after I saw my Harvard files came as a shock to me. In my present in-person state (well-aged), I bear little resemblance to the photos of my father that I've seen, and at the time I began my quest, the people who had known him told me that I did not look much like him. But when I gazed upon my beginning-year college photo and compared it with the picture of my father Aunt Verna had sent me (he was also beginning college at the time his photo was taken), I did a double-take. This drove home to me that I was this man's son. A picture indeed can be worth a thousand words.

The rest of my Harvard files read much like my Andover files, and my academic record accelerated past my just-good-enough Andover performance. In this regard, I was amused to see a frank comment from the Harvard admissions officer who evaluated my performance at Andover: "No one says he is an outstanding boy, but everyone says he has something above the average." In college, after I began studying social and developmental psychology, my interests in scholarly work

My father at start of college

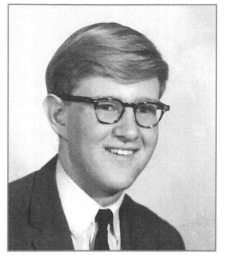

Myself at start of college

caught fire. I was pleased to see commendations by my senior year adviser, the great social psychologist Roger Brown: "Mr. Damon is an original, inventive, and independent student. . . . I tried to persuade him to enter our graduate program here, but he has chosen to go to Berkeley. This is a loss to us because he is going to do major work." I graduated magna cum laude and was inducted into Phi Beta Kappa.

Socially, my dorm proctor Bruce Babbitt (later to become a popular Arizona governor and secretary of the interior) gave me credit for "diverse interests," "overflowing enthusiasm," and "a good personality that carried him into many circles of students and junior faculty." I was also pleased to see an idealistic statement that I myself wrote about my life plans: "Man's purpose must be to reach higher and higher standards of morality and brotherhood." I do still hold this, though I've learned over the years to express such sentiments in gender-inclusive ways.

Reading over my school and college files with an eye toward my father's, I find both points of sharp contrast and points of intriguing similarities. Of course this can be said of comparisons between any two people: the human mind is an efficient sorting machine and can readily construct analogies and contrasts. In my case, though, I find the comparisons informative. They have revealed to me key factors that shaped my own character development, bringing me a clearer sense of how my own particular pattern of strengths and limitations evolved and how this bears on who I am and where I am heading.

The most obvious contrast between my father's school record and mine is his repeated failures as a student compared with my increasing successes. It's important to keep this contrast in perspective: academic success certainly does not tell us everything about the course of a life. The world is full of people who have failed in school and done brilliantly in their careers, and it is full of student stars who go on to do little in life or worse. In my father's case, as we shall see, he had much to be proud of in his military and government service after college. Schooling is but one phase of life.

Yet schooling matters. It offers skills and knowledge that prepare us to do good work, and it provides a training ground for character strengths such as diligence, purpose, attentiveness, and responsibility. It also matters while it's happening. Most people spend between fifteen and twenty years in school, and that's a good chunk of their life spans. All other things being equal, people who adjust well to school have something to feel fortunate about.

A likely explanation for the contrast between me and my father in our performances at the same school and college is that he had a privileged and overindulged childhood, whereas I was raised in a home with very little in the way of indulgence. As a consequence, I became more ambitious than he out of sheer need. There is certainly truth to this. I recall feeling a hunger to improve my situation early in childhood, well before my time at Andover; I also recall feeling fortunate and happy to be at Andover, unlike my father, and unlike my friends there who had more propitious home situations. In my day, it was seen as cool to complain about the school, and many of the complainers tended to be higher-status students. Despite the social appeal of doing this, I never could bring myself to speak ill of a place that I saw as a welcoming, almost heaven-sent, door to my future aspirations.

Unlike my father, I found purpose in the learning contexts of my school years. But the character trait that most stands out in our schoolboy contrasts is his unceasingly irresponsible behavior. He shirked his academic assignments, he faked illnesses to get out of work, and he disappointed teachers and parents who invested in him heavily—including his own father, who vigorously stood up for him even while ailing from a deadly disease.

How, I wonder, could my father have disappointed his loved ones in this way? With little family of my own, and few people to stick up for me, I learned to take responsibilities seriously. His easy start in life offered him too few opportunities to learn responsibility. The record of his parents' disappointment are preserved, like insects in ancient amber, in the anguished letters that his parents wrote to the school and that still sit in those rarely touched steel cabinets.

As my mother was to discover, my father did not completely outgrow his irresponsibility when he left his school days behind. In at least one area of his future life—being a father to me, his first child—his irresponsibility continued. I must agree with what my Aunt Verna (who loved him dearly) said to me, in her plain New England way: "That was not all right."

But life has a way of presenting new opportunities for everyone. When the call of service beckoned young Americans at the start of World War II, my father rose to the challenge. His life quickly became far less easy. Starting in that service, and afterward in others, he developed a sense of responsibility that would make a real difference to the world beyond himself. In his wartime military service, my father entered a territory that was unfamiliar to him, a territory full of hardships and troublesome drama that nothing had prepared him for. Eventually, he took on his; and he acquired grit, in the way Angela Duckworth has described in her groundbreaking book of that name. From the cauldron of real-world challenges suddenly thrust upon him at age nineteen, my father forged improved and sturdier elements of character.

5

National Service and Moral Maturity

"I DON'T KNOW why you want to dig up all that dirt."

These dampening words came from my Uncle Richard, my mother's younger brother. I was visiting him and his wife, Phyllis—both in their nineties, in good health with full mental capacities—in the hope that they would fill some of the gaps in my knowledge regarding what happened to my father. My mother had been dead for five years, and Richard was my one remaining family member with a link to that past.

Richard was resistant, to say the least, but I pressed him.

"I don't necessarily see my father's story—whatever it is—as dirt. I want to know what happened when he chose not to come back to the States after the war."

"It was that military trial," Richard muttered. "He had to testify."

"Nuremberg?" I blurted out, predictably, since Nuremberg was the iconic military trial that I had learned about in my history classes.

Richard mouthed an inaudible "no" and went silent after that. I couldn't tell whether his memory was failing him or whether he had simply had enough of this conversation. But unexpectedly, Aunt Phyllis came to the rescue. "It was Lichfield, wasn't it?" Richard begrudgingly nodded yes.

That was all I was able to get out of that visit, but it was enough. That one city's name—Lichfield—was new to me, but it would prove to be the key that opened the door to a chapter in my father's national service, and our country's history, that I knew nothing about. That chapter revealed to me a whole new side of who my father was—or, to put it more precisely, who he became once he left his lackadaisical school days behind and enlisted in the army for wartime service.

In my life-review mission to discover how my life was influenced by the father I never knew, the information I uncovered about his service to our country was invaluable. I was able to gain a sense of his life after I was conceived, and this helped me better understand why he failed to return home to my mother and me. It also gave me a picture of his character that was quite different from the one he showed during his school years.

He was never a saint, of course: his act of abandoning his wife and son remained as much in character as the principled behavior he displayed when serving his country. Like most people, he was complex, with an incongruous mix of admirable and faulty character traits. I found things in his life to admire, things to forgive, and things that still irk me. I'm not sure that I ever will be able to resolve these mixed feelings into a serene emotional state, but now at least I can identify them for what they are. This is an improvement over my earlier states of confusion, uncertainty, and submerged resentment. Understanding what really happened in my father's life has helped me ground my own life in a firm reality that was previously obscured from me. It has connected me with my actual family history—and, beyond that, with world history as well. I now can place myself in the order of things with a certainty I had never before felt.

Before that visit to my aunt and uncle, my research had uncovered the basic facts about my father's time in the military. He enlisted in US Army intelligence in October 1942, when he was a sophomore in college, leaving behind his aimless days as an indolent student and taking on the grim and serious challenges that come with military service. The year 1942 was the darkest year of the war. There was great uncertainty about prospects for victory against the well-organized forces of the Axis powers (Germany, Italy, Japan). The young men and women who signed up for US military service faced fearsome armies that had captured large segments of Europe, the Middle East, and the South Pacific. Despite the stalwart resistance of besieged countries such as England and Russia, no one really knew if the formidable Axis powers could be stopped.

I have no way of knowing whether patriotism played a role in my father's decision to sign up for the war, but certainly he must have been aware that, like every other military recruit at that time, he might end up sacrificing his life for his country. Whatever his reasons for enlisting, it seems clear to me that this decision started an entirely new chapter in his life, a chapter characterized by dedication to standards of liberty and equality and moral ideals such as truth and justice. His wartime military service and subsequent State Department service brought out in him a moral maturity that he had never previously displayed.

After his enlistment and basic training, my father was sent to an army training program to learn German. For the next two years, he served in radio intelligence on the European front. The specific details of his activities during those years have been lost to history, but it seems likely that, like others in his division (the 135th Radio Signal Corps), he decoded German radio messages from mobile stations near the front lines. This kind of work, like low-level spy work of all kinds, is boring but risky. There's a real danger of discovery and attack during the long hours of weeding through radio chatter in rickety undercover vehicles.

Toward the close of the war, my father was assigned to be a temporary guard at a military detention center for misbehaving US troops in England. Why he was given this brief assignment is not known; it lasted for only a few weeks in 1944. But it was through this posting that he found his way into the history books, where decades later, the son he left behind would be able to read about his testimony in a high-profile military trial with enduring consequences for the US military justice system.

Wartime Trials

"Philip Damon Lichfield." As soon as I typed these words into my internet search box, up popped a book title: *Blueberry Pie: The Meaning of WWII for the Americans Who Fought in It*. It was a memoir written by a distinguished historian, Otis Pease, near the end of his life.

When I looked up the historian's credentials, my heart stopped for a moment. Pease had taught at *Stanford*, of all places. I could have walked across campus to meet with him. But he died in 2010, barely two years before I began my search.

Pease would have been an amazing source. He grew up in Pittsfield, like my father, and the two knew each other as boys. When Pease was stationed in London at the end of the war, he ran into my father in an army canteen. This encounter made enough of an impression on Pease to be included in his wartime diary, which many years later became the book that I found on the internet. Here's the first part of what Pease wrote:

> I met Phil Damon (from Pittsfield) on detached service from Signal Corps to testify in the Lichfield Trials. Phil has become a Harvard-man-about-town tempered by the Army . . . the "trials" referred to here were part of an Army investigation into the notoriously harsh treatment of American GIs serving prison time in the Lichfield (Staffordshire) 10th Replacement Depot stockade for criminal offenses under the Articles of War.

The date of this entry in Pease's diary was November 21, 1945. I was barely a year old. Back home in Brockton, my mother was raising me with the help of her uncle and aunt. That past summer, we had spent a month visiting with my father's parents at their home in Pittsfield. Clearly, at that point, everyone expected my father to return to his family after his "detached service" for testifying at the trials was completed. What happened during his extended layover in Europe that may have persuaded him not to come back? What did he do at the trials, and what was his state of mind at the time? These were the questions that drove my search, as I began to dig for further information on the Lichfield Trials.

Lichfield, England, is a small city near the industrial hub of Birmingham. In the latter years of the Second World War, it became the site of the main staging post for American troops arriving on the European front. At a Victorian-era red-brick barracks complex known (in typical army-ese) as "The 10thReplacement Depot at Lichfield," US troops were prepared for battle. The complex included a detention center for GIs who misbehaved in minor ways (such as going AWOL for an evening and getting drunk in town). The GIs imprisoned at Lichfield were low-level enlisted men mostly from modest backgrounds. Some came from rural parts of the country, others from the inner city; some were Caucasian, others African American. At first, the detention center was a negligible postscript to the massive US Army staging post that contained it. In the end, it would garner such notoricty it overshadowed the main event.

It was not until 1945, the final year of the war, when army authorities began noticing something wrong at Lichfield. The story was first broken by Corporal Robert Henney of Toledo, Ohio, a young temporary guard in the detention center. When he returned home in January 1945, Corporal Henney called in a distressing report about the harsh treatment of Lichfield detainees to his local newspaper, the *Toledo Blade*. Henney told the *Blade* that he had observed guards at Lichfield mercilessly beating a GI with a rubber hose while the GI screamed in agony. When Corporal Henney tried to intervene, the guards threatened him rather than stopping their abuse.

Due to wartime censorship, the *Toledo Blade* was not allowed to run the story. But the newspaper's editor passed it along to a congressman, who in turn informed top army officials of the incident. The army investigated and determined that one guard, a sergeant with an otherwise unblemished record, should be prosecuted on a charge of mistreating GIs under his command.

The accused sergeant was brought up on charges of committing the following seven "cruel and inhuman disciplinary treatments" of GIs under his control: (1) forcing them to run double-time for up to two hours with their noses and feet up against a wall; (2) forcing them to eat an excess amount of food, followed by castor oil to purge the food; (3) placing them in a room without proper lighting for long periods; (4) ordering them to scrub floors outdoors without proper clothing in poor weather; (5) forcing them to extend their arms and hold them in constraining positions for long periods; (6) forcing them to eat cigarettes; (7) causing other unnecessary and extreme discomfort to the prisoners.

After a lengthy trial, the sergeant was convicted. But this was just the start of the story. As the trial progressed, it became clear that this one sergeant's treatment of prisoners was only the tip of the iceberg. What began as the trial of one errant sergeant became an investigation of a systemic policy of deliberate maltreatment carried out by the detention center guards and supported by their commanding officers.

Most shocking was the revelation that the proclaimed official policy at Lichfield was to treat GI detainees so severely that they would never again be tempted to disobey army rules or otherwise shirk their duty. The officers who ordered this policy believed that wartime soldiers must be made to fear the prospect of punishment so deeply that their fear would overwhelm their natural fear of battle—a rationale that was defended by battle-hardened career military officers who had seen cases of soldiers going AWOL or otherwise disobeying minor army rules in order to get themselves removed from the battlefront. Indeed, a major visiting Lichfield once complained that the detention center's treatment of prisoners was actually *too soft*: "You're not tough enough on these men, Sergeant," the major was quoted as saying. "You're running a hotel."

Whatever the merits of such battlewise concerns, it's clear that at Lichfield the punishment was not only strict but often cruel and vicious. The punishments were far and away disproportionate to the common infractions for which the GIs were detained, such as returning to the barracks late or inebriated after a night on the town. The punitive measures severely injured many prisoners and resulted in at least one death.

The duration of the yearlong, increasingly complex Lichfield Trials explains my father's absence through the end of 1946. Clues can be found in documents that reveal something of his experience during the time when he was a witness at these trials. Something of his character can be inferred from the documents as well.

The trial's initial venue was a bare-bones courtroom in the heart of London. There, the proceedings overflowed with anger on all sides. The prosecution was outraged by the testimonies of violent beatings, deprivations, harsh demands, and threats that had been directed at soldiers who were unlucky enough to find themselves detained in Lichfield. These soldiers were young men from underprivileged backgrounds and, with little worldly experience, knew little about how to protest or defend themselves from such attacks.

The defense expressed as much outrage as the prosecution. How could soldier-guards who were simply following their officers' orders be dragged through the humiliation of a court-martial? One of the officers who issued orders demanding harsh treatment of prisoners showed his disdain for the proceedings through intentional histrionics, described in the following way by an observer: "He was on the stand for five hours. Fourteen times in those five hours the president of the court had to bang his gavel to bring him to order. Once, in fact, he got so angry that he stuck out his tongue at [the president] like a child."

Witnesses for the prosecution reported receiving threats from partisans of the defense, including from the guards who were liable for prosecution. These guards had access to the quarters where the witnesses were stationed, and they did not hesitate to make it clear that they could take revenge on any witnesses whose testimony got them in trouble. Five of the witnesses became so intimidated by such threats that they refused their orders to testify. After sizing up the situation, the army responded by moving the trials out of England to a hotel in the small German town of Bad Nauheim, far from the British post where the threatening guards were stationed.

What was my father's attitude during the high-stress dramatics of the Lichfield Trials' London chapter? Here is Otis Pease's account of an evening out in London at just that time:

> I then met Phil Damon and took a bus with him to the Churchill Club in some magnificent old buildings behind Westminster. This is an elite American organization with some beautifully furnished English rooms. Phil moves in the educated upper circles of the army. . . . He has had three years at Harvard, is married, with one kid. We had a fair dinner and sherry with British officers and U.S. T/5s [corporal technicians] with PhDs. Upstairs later in a plush room furnished with conspicuous chandeliers, we discussed the poor situation in Germany—the bungling and the incompetence, the easy deal for officers. Where are there trained Americans for such service? Phil is fond of Army life in Paris and London and enthuses over the English. We agreed on the pettiness of some aspects of home and college. We then moved on to Sloane Square to a sharply contrasting pub, sleazy and crowded, full of various characters he met in his enthusiasm for London. Two beers made everything quite acceptable. We walked back to Washington Club, discussing English women.

This account, like a well-worked poem, contains multitudes. Pease's description of my father was off the cuff, not the stuff of carefully crafted analysis. But I believe that I'm on solid ground in taking away the following insights into my father's attitudes and goals at this pivotal time of his life.

First, and most captivating for me, it's evident that my father was telling people that he was "married, with one kid" a full year after I was born. He wasn't running away from this, at least then. This dispels the speculation that my father may have so keenly regretted his "mistake" in getting my mother pregnant that he determined to get out of the situation at the outset. It does not tell whether he felt "tricked" into the marriage, as Aunt Verna conjectured, or even whether he had serious doubts about the marriage. But my father's revelation that he had a wife and child does mean, as his army service wound down, that he was accepting his new family situation and that he likely intended to return home to it.

Yet the seeds of his eventual alienation from the home front are also apparent in Pease's passage. He eagerly joined Pease in complaints about "the pettiness of some aspects of home and college." In this regard, I wonder if he misled Pease about the number of his years at Harvard: he actually had just one, not three years, and that one year was far from a success. Did my father's uninspired record at college add an edge to his complaining?

Most telling are Pease's comments about my father's fondness for army life in Paris and England and his enthusiasm for London. My father must have drawn a contrast in his mind between provincial Massachusetts (a far more parochial place in those days) and sophisticated, cosmopolitan Europe. Pease's concluding comment about their shared interest in English women reminded me of the school reports describing my father as "girl-crazy." Was his roving eye during his London sojourn an early sign of a desire to expand his romantic horizons beyond the woman whom he had hastily married at the very young age of twenty-one?

I came away from reading Pease's account with a sense of my father as a youthful, high-spirited American soldier charmed by the thrills of European life. This was a familiar pattern for many small-town American men who found themselves exploring the streets of Paris, Rome, or London after their wartime fighting was done. During that brief, shining moment, Americans were received as heroes, on the side of the angels. Europeans had a rich culture with glittering worldly pleasures to share with the soldiers who had crossed the ocean to rescue the Old World from tyranny. How could a young man *not* have a good time under those conditions?

But unlike many of his fellow soldiers, my father's duties did not stop with the end of the war. He was thrown into the midst of a raging conflict of another sort, one that included frightening threats of retribution and physical violence. Yet, still, Pease took note of my father's "enthusiasm for London"! For me, this raises key questions about the characterological makeup of this man. How did he tune out the horrors of the trial he was immersed in? Was it courage that enabled him to get through this period with what Hemingway called "grace under pressure"? Or was it something else, in his nature, in his upbringing, and ultimately in his character? He was always one to take things lightly, way back to his school days. Was his unruffled demeanor at the time of the Lichfield Trials a reflection of his laid-back personality in general, or was it a function of his moral certainty regarding the inhumane behavior he was called to testify about? From my professional awareness of the complexity of people's motivations when faced with difficult circumstances, I would speculate that both factors were at play.

Unlike the five intimidated witnesses who begged off, my father did testify. In fact, his testimony became remarkably prominent in news accounts, considering his short-term experience at Lichfield. My father was one of three witnesses quoted in a definitive piece on Lichfield in a military magazine called *After the Battle*. In the midst of the article's extensive coverage of the courtroom drama—complete with over a dozen photos of the grim surroundings—I found the following paragraph:

> Additional damning testimony was given by PFC Philip A. Damon of Pittsfield, Massachusetts, a former Harvard student. "Most of the prisoners," he said, "were pretty good boys who had been wounded in combat and rebelled against the Army's refusal to let them see

town before shipping them back to the front." Damon admitted that he hadn't witnessed any beatings himself but said that some of the prisoners in the work details had shown him welts on their backs where they had been flogged.

In addition to the comprehensive *After the Battle* article, there is one other authoritative source of information about the trials. Lieutenant Jack Gieck attended the first sessions when he was stationed in London as an army officer. Forty years later, unable to get the experience out of his mind, Gieck decided to write the book *Lichfield: The U.S. Army on Trial*. The book has just one quote by my father, but it is a good one: "Private Philip Damon quoted a slogan used by the guards: 'Your soul may belong to God, but your body belongs to me.'"

The US Army command, to its credit, declared that threatening GIs with inhumane treatment was not an appropriate way to obtain obedience, nor was it a effective way to inspire loyalty and bravery in battle. The message came from the top. Dwight David Eisenhower, Chief of Command in Europe at the time, was a plainspoken and no-nonsense general known for his cordial relations with enlisted soldiers. Eisenhower insisted on a thorough investigation of the Lichfield complaints. In so doing, he bucked army tradition: this was the first time in history that the US Army had investigated itself.

By the end of August 1946, the Lichfield Trials concluded with the conviction of Col. James A. Kilian and other officers for permitting the brutal handling of American inmates. The conviction of the officers was what the prosecution was aiming for: it would have been a travesty of justice to leave all the blame with low-level enlisted men who were taking their orders from the Lichfield detention center's command. This set an admirable direction for the US military that has persisted to this day.

The article concluded:

The Lichfield case played an important role in changing the American Army's code of military justice. Congress launched an investigation into the entire court-martial system and concluded it had been unduly harsh and arbitrary during the war. . . . By 1951, Congress had revised the code of military law from end to end.

Eisenhower, with the active encouragement of President Harry Truman, oversaw these reforms. Soon after, he went on to become a widely respected American president, leading the country through a period of peace and prosperity under tense international conditions. The Cold War required a firm and steady hand, vigilance, and a wholehearted dedication to the bedrock American principle of liberty. Eisenhower met this challenge with quiet but forceful confidence. Accordingly, my father's destiny was shaped by the moral choices that Eisenhower made during and after the war. Little noticed and far away, my destiny too was indirectly fashioned by these choices.

Although largely forgotten today outside the obscure domain of military history, the Lichfield Trials were widely reported in the newspapers and popular magazines of the time, with passionate editorial commentary decrying the abuse of common soldiers who had fought in our country's battles and had done nothing much wrong. There were stories in *Time*, *Life*, the *Saturday Evening Post*, and all the major newspaper chains. There was coverage in African American newspapers of the day because among the mistreated soldiers were a number of young Black recruits. My father's hometown paper, the *Berkshire Eagle*, ran a front-page story of his testimony, accompanied by a photograph of him in uniform. That picture shows a stern, "gritty," war-hardened visage bearing little resemblance to the sweet, amiable face that appeared in my father's school-days portraits.

The *Berkshire Eagle* coverage revealed an additional dimension to the story. My father, it turned out, had been writing home to his own father about the brutal conditions in the detention center, because he hoped "people at home could do something about the conditions." His letters, however, were intercepted by army censors. My father's commanding

My father, a hardened young soldier, breaking grim news to the *Pittsfield Berkshire Eagle*

officer warned him that the letters were "a breach of security because they cast discredit on the U.S. Army." The story in the *Berkshire Eagle* does not date the letters or the commanding officer's reprimand. The date of the story itself is January 8, 1946, barely a month after the trial began. In the early days of the trial, my father reported the censorship. At the trial, he quoted his commanding officer as saying, "What goes on in Lichfield is supposed to remain here."

The *Berkshire Eagle* story notes that "Damon went to England in the fall of 1944." It seems that my father was writing home about conditions at Lichfield even before the scandal was made public by Corporal Henney's January 1945 communication to the *Toledo Blade*. If that indeed was the case, my father showed a true moral sense by taking the initiative to alert people at home so that they might, in his words, "do something about the conditions." In the face of the censors and his commanding officer's orders, he also showed genuine courage—and compassion—by sticking with his purpose of telling the truth about what he had discovered.

My father paid a price for his truth-telling. By 1944, before his assignment at Lichfield, he had risen in rank from corporal to sergeant. Yet in his discharge in 1946, he was listed as private first class. Although there's no existing record of this, it is reasonable to surmise that this demotion was due to my father's violation of the censorship regulations. Fortunately, this punishment did not have a long-term effect on his career: after the war, he went on to secure prestigious posts in the War Department and State Department. I am guessing that my father's courageous truth-telling was recognized by government officials and that they rewarded him for his principled behavior by hiring him for the positions he sought.

The last line of the *Berkshire Eagle* story about my father's testimony reads as follows: "He is married to the former Miss Helen Meyers of Brockton, and they have a son, William Van Buren Damon." There it is. No matter where my father's mind was in those days, I existed!

Character Development in Adulthood

My research into the Lichfield Trials and my father's part in them transformed my view of his character. Against all expectations, I discovered that my father displayed moral conviction in a tense and consequential historic situation. He was a courageous truth-teller. He demonstrated compassion for soldiers who were suffering unheard and acted on this compassion in the face of warnings from powerful higher-ups who gave him the message that they wanted him to remain silent. His refusal to do so benefited our country and its code of military justice. At this time in his young adulthood, my father found purpose in service to his country.

He also developed a hardiness of character that we nowadays call "grit." This is evident from the newspaper photograph of him as a hardened soldier at the time when he wrote home to report the prisoner abuse he witnessed, braving the stern directives of army censors. It is evident from Otis Pease's description of him as he began his Lichfield testimony. In the midst of threats emanating from the officers he would testify against, my father was resolute in his opposition to the inhumane acts. Unlike several of his peers, he never backed off his testimony. He never gave indications of being intimidated. He had become, to cite a highly valued trait of the time, *tough*.

At Andover and Harvard, toughness was seen as a crucial quality in a boy. This was still true by the time I was a student (my recommendation letter from Andover for college admissions made a point of noting that I was "tough enough"; this must have been all the more expected in my father's day). My father was *not* tough as a schoolboy; that was one of the focal points of his counselors' many criticisms of his character. It took a war to elicit toughness from him. He rose to the occasion in a morally heroic way.

My father was clearly not the no-account deadbeat that I had assumed him to be in my younger days, during those rare occasions when I

The improvised Army courtroom in Bad Nauheim, Germany, where the Lichfield Trials were transferred after witness threats in London

bothered to think about him at all. In my late-life discoveries, I've found myself pleased at revelations of his good values and his evident character strengths. In large part, I'm sure, this is because he was my father; and despite his permanent absence from my life I still have felt a tendency to identify with him. But, also, as a professional developmental psychologist I'm gratified to observe one more case of a person growing from a self-centered, indulgent youth to an adult of purpose and principle. In my work on purpose and moral commitment, I've always enjoyed such cases when I've come across them in my research. For obvious reasons, I reveled in this one.

Yet he abandoned his first wife (my mother) and his first child (me) without, as far as I know, any word of consolation, regret, or explanation. His abandonment of me was permanent. Lawan and Sumali told me of a time when they asked him about me, and he said that he didn't want to talk about anything related to me. Interestingly, my memory of what they first told me about this has my father sitting at dinner with his three children, and Pichitra asked, "What about this 'William' our Aunt Verna mentioned to us?" My father's response, in my recalled (but apparently errant) version of this story, was to slam his hand on the table and say, "We don't speak of William here!" But when I went over this account again with Lawan and Sumali while fact-checking for this book, they replied that there was never any hand slamming. I chalk this discrepancy up to the fallibilities and biases of my memory, as I discussed in chapter 1. Notably, the discrepancy reveals how emotionally charged the story of this incident was for me.

In my father's (non)relationship with me, the irresponsibility he showed during his school years remained an active feature of his character. I was not the only person affected by this. First and foremost, my mother was deeply and irrevocably hurt. Whatever joy I've had in discovering the character strengths that my father displayed at the Lichfield Trials is tempered by thoughts of my mother's anguish at his failure to come home.

There also were *his* mother and father, who already had ached for years over their son's irresponsibility at school. When he failed to come home, they were so distraught—and angry—that they broke off relations with him. My father was their treasured son, but abandoning a wife and child was an unacceptable breach in the New England Yankee culture they lived in. According to Aunt Verna, they informed my father that they no longer considered him part of the family. This family break was made even more heartbreaking by the death of my grandfather at age fifty. He was, of course, the father to whom my father wrote those letters about the Lichfield scandals. The two had an exceptionally warm and close relationship. Clearly my father depended on his father for support and guidance. Yet after my father's decision to stay in Europe, the two never spoke again. Over time, perhaps there might have been a reconciliation, as there eventually was between my father and grandmother. But my grandfather died too soon for this to happen, if it indeed ever would have been possible. What pain both men must have lived with for the entire time each had left on the planet!

Later in life, my father would share another misfortune with my grandfather. Both suffered from multiple sclerosis, and in their respective times each would die of that debilitating disease. MS is a condition that strikes at the prime of life. It is a cruel condition that occurs in sudden attacks that can damage the person's ability to walk, talk, and see. Some have mild versions that leave them relatively unaffected for decades. Not so, sadly, for my father and grandfather. When Aunt Verna told me of their fates, she moaned that "they just kept going straight down." My grandfather died at fifty, after fighting the disease for over ten years. My father lived until he was sixty-nine, but his last twenty years were spent bedridden in Thailand, in pain and unable to do much beyond listening to books on tape. The thought of my father and grandfather suffering so much causes me a sadness that's hard to bear. This reaction surprises me, because I never met my father in person and have only a dim recollection of seeing my grandfather when I was four. And I must admit that my first reaction when I found out about their shared disease was to look up whether or not it's genetic (it's not). But once this personal fear for myself and my children was calmed, deep sorrow kicked in, as if I had known my father and grandfather as part of my true family. My reaction is an indication of how vivid my family search and discoveries have become to me during my life review.

Character and moral commitment rarely develop overnight. Of course there have been some famous sudden conversions to the path of righteousness in human history. In a moment on the road to Damascus, Saint Paul was transformed from a zealous persecutor of the oppressed to a devoted advocate of compassion and justice. Developmental science has documented similarly dramatic conversion cases. But these are highly atypical. Most major changes in character and commitment come about slowly, over the course of many years.

People can change for the better. They can become more responsible when (and if) they mature. People can become committed to serious moral causes, even at significant personal cost. When this occurs, it almost always takes place step-by-step, gradually, over an extended period of time. The movement is often imperceptible at first. There is hesitation and resistance; there may be backsliding. Only after repeated actions and trials do lasting transformations take place. In my writings on moral development, I've described this uneven process as a "gradual transformation of goals," because over time it affects the person's most motivating aims in life.

As I noted in chapter 3, the master concept driving my professional work over the past two decades is purpose. My book *The Path to Purpose* shows how finding purpose is crucial for a successful transition to adulthood. Finding purpose bestows energy, motivation, resilience, and commitment to causes beyond the self. It can turn aimless, drifting adolescents into focused and high-achieving adults. This was exactly the growth I observed in my father's character. Within a decade, he went from a lackadaisical seventeen-year-old in 1939 to a man devoted to serving his country in an honorable fashion.

In my father's case, the effect of his military service in army radio intelligence no doubt was powerfully compounded by his testimony at the tensely consequential Lichfield Trials. I can imagine what it must have been like for a twenty-two-year-old ex-college student from a sheltered small-town New England home to participate in hearings with reports of GIs being ordered to stand undressed and rigidly at attention for hours in freezing weather, forced to march double-time up and down stairs to the point of collapse, and beaten bloody with clubs and hoses. Suddenly he was in a position to do something about this. He took a stand on the side of what he knew was right.

In the course of human development, unexpected and dramatic events can trigger the reflections and choices that in turn pave the way for the discovery of purpose and the subsequent transformation of identity. In my father's Foreign Service career, as I discuss in chapter 6, he became a voice of reason in the contentious climate of international conflict, and he pressed for civil rights just as that moral cause was rising to the level of national consciousness. The character strengths my father forged in the conflict and brutalities of World War II were to endure as he found new ways to pursue purpose in his later government career.

My father completed his military service and was honorably discharged from the army on July 10, 1946. Immediately after his discharge, while still testifying at the trials, he was hired as a civilian employee in the US War Department, which was beginning its occupation of postwar Germany. A *Galveston Daily News* story dated July 27, 1946, indicates that my father started working for the War Department less than two weeks after his discharge from the army. He would remain in his new job for four more years, serving in its German division. He did not return home. My mother waited in vain for him, as did his parents. My mother suffered what was called in those days a "nervous breakdown," as her cousin Gerry told me shortly before his own death. She did a good job of keeping her distress from me. In the haze of early childhood, I was unaware of anything unusual in her behavior.

Cousin Gerry, an attorney, filed divorce papers for my mother after it became clear that my father was never coming back. I have found no records of those papers or the date of their filing. A devout Roman Catholic, my mother applied for an annulment in the eyes of the Church on July 3, 1953. The archdiocese protocol declared that she received a "favorable decision from Rome in connection with the case."

For my life review, the facts I've uncovered about the background of my father's refusal to return home bring up the most resonant question of all: How would my life had turned out if my father, ignoring his strong desires out of a sense of responsibility, had returned to my mother and me? His heart clearly was in Europe at that time. Moral judgments aside, how would it have actually worked if he came back, feeling the way he did? My mother, for all her virtues, was not easy to get along with. Would our family have stayed together if my father had rejoined it? What would my childhood have been like amid the inevitable marital conflicts that would have ensued? What kind of a father would he have been for me? Would he have resented his family obligations? Would I have bristled under the hand of a resentful father? While I know I will never find definitive answers to these questions, the material I uncovered to enable these reflections has been an unquestionable benefit for my sense of self, my quest for positive and authentic identity, and my affirmation of the life I've been given.

6

Three Separate Paths to Purpose

IN THE SUMMER of 1963, when I was a student hitchhiking around Europe, I found myself in Munich one hot and hazy afternoon. Lonely and worn out from my bare-bones travel, I wandered the streets of that foreign city until a sign on a building caught my attention. It read "Amerikahaus." Intrigued, I entered and discovered that it was an American cultural center, with an open library and stacks full of current periodicals. I welcomed the comfortable, familiar-looking place to sit and read American magazines. After spending the afternoon in that hospitable atmosphere, I continued on my travels, revived and re-grounded. Little did I realize at the time that this was a point at which my life path and my father's intersected, albeit over a decade apart. It turns out that my father, wholly unknown to me, contributed to the creation of that place.

When the Lichfield trials wrapped up in August 1946, Philip Damon's duties as a witness were fulfilled. His honorable discharge from the army had come a month before that. There was nothing to prevent him from returning home other than his own desires. I was not yet two years old and had no awareness of his absence. But everyone else on the scene—my mother, his parents, his sister Verna—expected him back. Yet he stayed. With his refusal to come home, his life and my life went their separate ways.

In my life review, as I contemplated my father's choice not to return, two questions kept nagging at me. The questions were obvious, and unanswerable, but I could not sidestep them. What motivated my father to stay in Europe? And how would my life had been different had he come back to my mother and me?

Since I had no way of answering these questions with full facts, my only solution was to use the facts that I did have to create accounts of the lives most affected by my father's choice. Those lives were my father's, my mother's, and my own. What directions did each of our lives take after my father decided to stay in Europe in August 1946? Tracing the directions of the three lives could not answer my two questions directly, but it would give me material for educated guesses—what psychological scientists might call "informed speculations."

In this account, I use my father's postwar story as the pivot point against which to chart the directions my mother's life and mine took during the same period. I do this because it was my father who made the choice that resulted in the three of us going our separate ways. I admit as well to being fascinated by the colorful life my father led. It makes a great story. I can't speak for my mother, who is no longer with us, but my own story is more ordinary—interesting to me, of course, and full of its own modest dramas, challenges, and blessings. But my life has not been linked to great spectacles of history to anywhere near the extent my father's was. For these reasons, it is my father's story after the war that is the pivot-piece of this chapter.

Tracing the directions of our postwar lives also provided me with a conclusion that I wasn't anticipating but that turned out to be of special interest to me. The three of us, separately and in our own unique ways, pursued lifelong purposes that became central parts of our personal identities. Our purposes were different from one another—notably different, especially for people from the same (putative) family. This reflects the individual nature of purpose in general; but in our three cases, we took this individuality to an extreme.

As I've reviewed my life and the lives of the people who most influenced me, tracing these three paths has been an informative exercise. Among other things, it's confirmed for me the adaptability of the human spirit. Each of us can find a way, a unique and individual way. In some instances, we start by dealing the hand ourselves; in others, we play whatever cards we've been dealt. In all cases, the choices we make define our destinies.

My Father's Postwar Path to Purpose

In late 1946, the War Department took over the US occupation of Germany from the army. This was just around the time that my father made his own transition from the army to the War Department and, soon after, from the War Department to the State Department. Each transition reflected a turning from military to civilian missions. The War Department's initial mission was to place civilian German leaders in charge of that defeated country, replacing military authorities of the occupying powers (the United States, France, Great Britain, and the Soviet Union). After that, the occupying powers stayed around for a few years to oversee the civilian leadership that they had installed. During that time, their efforts evolved from military-backed police work to social, political, and cultural goals.

In service to these goals, my father assumed cultural and diplomatic roles working for the State Department. In 1948, he was listed in a State Department Foreign Service List as a "cultural officer" in the small town of Gross Gerau, next to Bad Nauheim (where he had been stationed for his Lichfield Trials testimony). Soon after Gross Gerau, my father was listed as a "program officer" in a State Department office in Berlin.

A later Foreign Service List reveals that he was a "cultural officer" in Waldeck-Wolfhagen on October 6, 1949, at a salary of $4,380 a year. The next month, his salary was increased to $5,370.

I have a good sense of my father's work in occupied Germany thanks to Iza Warner, the widow of Robert Warner, a State Department colleague of my father's. Iza, at age ninety-two, regaled me with stories of my father's diplomatic escapades. I came away from our meetings well informed about my father as a young diplomat in war-torn Germany.

Germany at the end of World War II was a rubble-ridden mess. Cities and factories were bombed out, food and heating fuel were scarce, and refugees from the neighboring countries that Germany had attacked wandered homeless through the land. Germany was in a "bicycle age": a period when automobiles were so unavailable to the general public that owning a bike could be literally lifesaving at times. Demoralized and wary, Germans looked at fellow citizens with suspicion and blame for the horrifying mistakes their country had made. "Apathy is widespread," wrote military reporter Julian Bach. "After twelve years of the worst dictatorship in history, they are not in good moral shape. After six years of the most destructive war in history, they are not in good physical shape. The cities are ruined, the cupboard is half-empty, the people are withered and spent." During that initial postwar period, people survived as best they could by bartering items such as cigarettes for precious rations of protein and calories. The military felt a need to issue sanctions against "fraternization" to protect German women from tempting inducements to prostitute themselves for coveted American cash and gifts. "Disrupted transportation, choked-up canals and rivers, smashed storage and processing facilities, a population made top-heavy by the influx of 4,000,000 extra mouths to feed . . . make the German food struggle an unending struggle against the aftermath of war and defeat," Bach wrote early in the occupation.

The mission of the US occupation of Germany was threefold. Its first goal was to make sure that all remaining German resistance was quelled, so that Germany was no longer a threat to peace—"to make certain that *the war stays won*," as a commanding officer proclaimed early in the occupation. This pacification goal was accomplished by the overwhelming military presence of the American army, combined with the passivity of the now-beaten-down German population.

The occupation's second goal was to restore the Germans' capacity to feed and clothe themselves, along with all the other benefits of a well-functioning economy. This goal too was accomplished before long, with help from the Marshall Plan, which provided generous American support for the reconstruction of German farms and factories. Once put back on their feet with this help, the German people rebuilt a thriving economy.

The occupation's third goal was less straightforward, because it aimed for cultural and psychological rather than military and material transformations. As Bach described it, the intent was "to 'recover' the German hearts and minds so that eventually, instead of Nazis, the Germans will be democrats, and Germany, instead of being a law-breaker among nations, will become a law-abiding member of the family of nations." This was a matter of social, cultural, and political change through the transmission of American ideals and culture. This kind of sociocultural transmission was to become my father's life work, at first in Germany and later in Asia.

In postwar Germany, the sociocultural mission began with eradicating Nazi doctrine from the legal, journalistic, artistic, and educational places where it had held sway. Jews, Roma, and Poles had been subject to different laws than the rest of the population. Hundreds of laws needed to be changed and dozens of judges fired. Materials needed to be written to retrain lawyers, judges, legal aides, and the police. Educational curricula for children had to be revised from the ground up. School textbooks during the Nazi regime were full of glorifications of world conquest through warfare and idealizations of the German soldier. They also contained diatribes against disfavored ethnic groups, political opponents, and foreign adversaries. The textbooks were effective: when the US military government took over, it found that German youth were the portion of the native population most dedicated to Nazi principles. "The kids are in a muddle," wrote Bach. "They find themselves holding onto a multitude of Nazi beliefs that were drummed into them. They've been taught to hate anything foreign in nature and admire only the achievements of the 'Master Race.'" The War Department went about this task with a resolve that matched its earlier efforts on the battlefield. Within three months, it authored twenty new schoolbooks and rushed more than five million copies into print. Schools were reopened, and two million German children were sent back to school. The textbook project continued through the 1940s, generating an entirely new catalog of readings for German students. Side by side with the book project came teacher training programs that introduced German schoolteachers to principles such as equal rights, democracy, and international cooperation.

For the adult population, the War Department sponsored cultural events highlighting American movies, artworks, and popular music. By 1947, it had opened over two hundred movie theaters in the American sectors of Germany, which could select from fifty American films, among which were Charlie Chaplin's *The Gold Rush* and Spencer Tracy's *The Young Thomas Edison*. The films had been chosen based on a stated policy of "showing the Germans the way we live, telling them a bit about our background and customs, and showing them our non-military way of life." German audiences must have enjoyed the films, because the movie theaters were packed.

There is a small space of difference between education and propaganda. It was within this space that my father operated. His War Department work informed the German population about the cultural and historical traditions of the United States. That was the educational part. At the same time, this work was designed to convert people to the values and principles of a free and democratic society. That part tips over into propaganda if the message relies on subtle persuasion and covert advocacy.

My father and his colleagues in the War Department must have had success in walking that line in a convincing way, because West Germany

became a model former dictatorship transformed into a thriving democratic republic with a powerful economy and American-style civil liber-
ties. It also became a close ally of the United States and in most matters
remained pro-American for the duration of the Cold War. My father's
War Department service played some part in this achievement.

Over time, this work took my father to a succession of German cities, including Munich and Frankfurt, and small towns, some of fewer
than a thousand inhabitants, moving every year or so. It was when he
was assigned to Kollmar in 1951 that he met Iza's husband, fellow diplomat Robert Warner. The couple were to become his closest friends
during his time in Germany and in Washington, DC, after that.

The main instrument of my father's cultural transmission work was
a set of "information centers" that the United States established throughout the American sector of occupied Germany. The United States built
the first of these centers in Wiesbaden and followed up with centers in
Frankfurt, Berlin, Heidelberg, Munich, Cologne, and many other places.
These centers adopted the name "Amerikahaus" (America House),
drawn from the results of a contest that asked visitors to propose names.
The Amerikahaus program became one of the premier international cultural promotion efforts sponsored by the United States in the mid-
twentieth century.

The Amerikahaus centers, like the one I strolled into in Munich,
contained libraries full of books, magazines, newspapers, and other periodicals that provided information about American culture and poli-
tics. The libraries were designed to be cheerful places to sit and read. In
addition to reading materials, they housed musical recordings of popular American genres such as jazz and Broadway show tunes. Visitors
could hear Count Basie and Buddy Rich on turntables and keep up with
the latest Rodgers and Hammerstein numbers. They could stay for
discussions about what they heard. In February 1949, the Giessen
Amerikahaus discussed the question "Is jazz supposed to be real artistic music?" The centers showed short films about subjects such as
American agriculture and geography, sponsored lectures by scholars who
were traveling nearby in Europe, and offered pleasant spaces for card

games, poetry readings, and singing groups. A 1950 report estimated that over one million Germans frequented one or more of the centers each year. The centers were popular with German youth in particular.

My father was no more than a mid-level official at Amerikahaus. He never appears in any of the existing photos of the program's leadership. But according to Aunt Verna and Iza, he was there from the beginning, and while he had no authority over operations, he was a key player in arranging cultural events across the centers. Although my father never finished college, he had the interests, bearing, and reputation of an intellectual. Officials in the War Department and the State Department paid attention to him on cultural matters. A combination of low-level authority and marked influence—an influence implemented through persuasion and example—was to characterize my father's vocational status throughout his career.

For the United States and the other Allied powers, the reconstruction of Germany was an enormous task, and not always an orderly one. My father, like many government employees in Germany at that time, was shifted from assignment to assignment as the needs of the occupation evolved. Iza recalls that Robert and my father found themselves "in charge" of small German towns that were establishing Nazi-free local governments. Robert and my father screened the German officials by investigating their records and getting to know them over informal dinners that Iza prepared in their home. "We were sifting through German officials, weeding out the real Nazis, choosing ones likely to be pro-American rather than communists," Iza said. As a Parisian who suffered through the Nazi invasion, Iza disliked entertaining Germans who may have been ex-Nazis, but she did it anyway, with her signature graciousness.

Iza told me that my father loved Germany. She remembers him saying that most Germans were not Nazis and in fact disliked the Nazis as much as anyone did. My father's love of Germany set the stage for the highly successful work he did for the Amerikahaus program in his budding diplomatic career. His warmth toward the Germans, Iza said

My father, a young diplomat in postwar Germany, with Iza and her daughters

with a smile, was right in character, because "he was a fun-loving man with a wonderful sense of humor—and he did enjoy people so!" One sign of my father's diplomatic success in Germany, she told me, was that, when he was assigned to be the American official overseeing the town of Passau, the people there voluntarily named him their honorary mayor. I have not had an opportunity to find out whether there is any record of this in Passau, but if I ever make it there, I will certainly visit its town hall to see if some trace of this honor still exists.

For my life review, the discovery of my father's early career success in Germany, along with his evident joy in living there, gave me an answer to my most pressing question about why he never came back. In a vocational sense, he had found his calling: the work he did for the State Department matched his abilities, his interests, and his empathic disposition. The work provided him a meaningful way to serve his country's interests while also contributing to the recovery of the German populace that had been devastated by a calamitous war. What's more, my father had a blast living in that sophisticated old-world setting, a sharp contrast to the parochial culture of his New England youth. He was doing good work and having fun, a combination hard to resist. As I imagined him as a fun-loving young man in his twenties living this charmed life, I stopped wondering why he stayed over there despite the loss of his family ties. My life review satisfied my nagging curiosity about this, which I found to be a significant and lasting relief.

My father's fun-loving side was blended with the frivolous irresponsibility that remained from his schoolboy days—which also helps account for his decision to remain in Germany without assuming his marital and parental duties. Iza described him as "charmingly unruly." As in his school days, he continued to be neglectful about day-to-day matters. He often forgot his appointments. In today's vocabulary, he was laid-back. Sometimes when he sent a letter, he would just write the person's name and the town on the envelope, counting on the post office to figure out the right address. Once, when writing a letter to Iza's aunt, for example, he simply addressed it to "*Tante* Marie, Wiesbaden." Incredibly, Marie got the letter.

Iza recalled that she first met my father when Robert invited him to their home for dinner. Iza prepared her usual elegant cuisine, but my father forgot to come. It took her a long time to forgive him for this: "I said to Robert that night, 'Don't ever invite that man back for dinner; I am not cooking for him again!'" In time, however, Iza put my father back on her dinner list. Yet at age ninety-two, she still remembered his lapse vividly, with a mix of irritation and good-humored exasperation.

My father, Iza recalled, "had no filter." He was spontaneous and unreserved. This made him charmingly amusing when he told off-the-cuff jokes. It also often placed him on the verge of trouble—a "devilish" young man, as Iza put it, always out to have a good time. His apartment was a mess (Iza remembered chairs with only three out of four legs and orange crates used for tables), and he was rarely there. He was usually out meeting people, seeing the sights, philandering. Robert, she said, was a stabilizing influence on him, not always effective but still needed. As she spoke, my mind flashed back to the discoveries I had made in my search through his school records. The same pattern of friendly gregariousness, fun-loving humor, easygoing living habits, and a bit of recklessness obviously endured beyond his childhood days. So too did his casual attitude toward responsibilities and social conventions.

Then, with a surge of feeling that surprised me, I recalled the family pictures that Aunt Verna shared with me on my first visit. Several of them showed my father snuggling in his father's lap, a happy dreamlike expression on his young face. I remembered too what Verna had told me (also reflected in his school records) about the extreme level of attention my father received from their parents (especially their mother) when he was young. At that moment, I realized that one of my father's distinguishing characteristics was his steady sense of self-confidence, engendered by his extremely secure and affectionate upbringing. This, I knew from my own professional field, was Child Development 101: secure attachments in the early years of life ground people in a self-confidence that enables them to explore the world, take risks, go out on limbs, and vigorously seek new relationships.

When affectionate parenting extends beyond secure attachments to overindulgence, however, patterns of behavior that are less adaptive can emerge. The type of irresponsibility, indolence, and lack of self-discipline that my father displayed throughout his youth is typical of children who have been excessively indulged by caring, well-meaning parents. In such cases, the benefits of self-assuredness may be counterbalanced by deficits in diligence and restraint.

How different from my own life experience, I thought. As a child, I had no taste of that dreamy sense of security that I read on my father's childhood face. Until my life review, I never realized how much I must have craved it. At the same time, my life review also made me aware of the character strengths I was able to acquire because I needed to strive for benefits that had come so easily to my father. My gratitude for this eased the sting of my envy for the warm and constant parenting that my father enjoyed. This dose of gratitude was a direct result of my life review, squarely in keeping with a life review's agenda of finding affirmation through positive sentiments such as gratitude.

Iza remembers a lunch she had with my father and one of her close friends early in her acquaintance with him. The conversation was mostly small talk, nothing special in the way of intimate disclosures or fascinating revelations. But soon after they parted, my father phoned Iza and asked her to find out if her friend would like to marry him! Astonished, Iza told my father that his request was "stupid" and she would do no such thing. This curious incident, combined with my father's dinner faux pas, gave Iza a first impression of him as a reckless, immature, uncivilized fool. But over time she forgave his foolish behavior and came to appreciate his more attractive qualities.

It was a good thing for my father that Iza eventually did forgive him, because she turned out to play a role in his second marriage. Through a mutual friend, Iza was introduced to Genevieve Lespagnol, a young ballerina starring in a new Jean Cocteau ballet called *La Dame à la Licorne*. Genevieve sent Iza three tickets to the ballet, which featured Genevieve as a noble maiden who owns a white unicorn that eats from her hand. The maiden has an affair with a handsome knight, after which the unicorn refuses to eat and dies. The maiden, bereaved, loses interest in the knight, and as the final curtain falls, she is onstage alone, with neither knight nor unicorn, pointing to a sign that reads "*Mon seul désir*" (my only desire). Cocteau wrote this tragic tale in 1953, and it premiered in Munich, where Robert, Iza, and my father were stationed at the time. Iza gave her extra ticket to my father, and after the performance she invited Genevieve to join the three of them for dinner.

The rest, as they say, is history. Within a year, my father proposed to Genevieve, and she accepted, becoming Genevieve Damon. My father did not hide his less-than-conscientious ways from his new love. When the rattletrap of a car he owned at the time was stolen just days before their wedding, he told his bride-to-be, "The only possessions I had were a car and a toothbrush. Now I only have the toothbrush." Genevieve clearly did not marry my father for his money. His good nature, his intelligence, and his charm must have won her over.

A final relic from my father's days in Germany passed down to me upon the death of my Aunt Verna. As her son Chris was cleaning out his mother's attic, he came upon a small box of books my father had given her before he left Germany for his new assignment in Thailand. (At that time, Verna and her husband were living in Europe too.) One of the books caught my attention: *The Double Axe*, a book of poetry by Robinson Jeffers, a Californian known for his impassioned (and prescient) advocacy for environmental preservation. What I did not know until seeing *The Double Axe* was that Jeffers was also a radical isolationist. He wrote in the preface to his book, "I think it will become equally clear that our intervention in the Second World War has been—even terribly— worse in effect [than World War I]." The book was published in 1947, right on the heels of the war that killed more than four hundred thousand US troops. The book's publisher, Random House, felt so uncomfortable with Jeffers's position on the war that it noted at the beginning of the book its "disagreement over some of the political views pronounced by the poet in this volume," a statement of disavowal that may stand alone in the annals of poetry publishing.

What was my father doing with this book? He surely was an internationalist, then and in his later career. But he had testified against military violence and brutality in the recent Lichfield Trials, and in later years he was to express admiration for Martin Luther King, Jr. Did my father admire the book for its pacifist sentiments? Did Jeffers's poetic protests influence him? Or was he simply reading the poems out of intellectual and aesthetic interests?

There is no way to know. But one thing can be known: *the book did not actually belong to him.* It belonged to the "U.S. Army, Nurnberg Post," according to stampings on several of its pages. My father must have borrowed it from the army library and never bothered to return it. Well, there he goes again.

The part of my life review that has focused on my father's time in Germany led me to the stunning realization that I very likely did better in life by finding my own way through childhood than I would have by growing up in the midst of a troubled family with a resentful father who likely would have been looking back at a highly appealing life well suited to his interests, skills, and personality. In addition, at that age, he was hardly the model of paternal responsibility. I wouldn't go so far as to give credit to my father for making the best choice on my behalf, but I would say that his stay in Germany may have turned out to have been the best available outcome for both of us. I'll return to this insight in the final chapter of this book. For now, I'll just note that, since one of the hoped-for outcomes of a life review is gratitude for the life we've been given, this realization in itself made my discovery quest worthwhile.

My Father's Service in Thailand

When my father was transferred to Thailand in 1954, the country was considered "small, weak, and underdeveloped" by the US government. Rural and mostly poor, almost 90 percent of the population farmed or mined, producing rice, rubber, tin, and teak products. Thailand's one major urban center was Bangkok, a steamy jumble of huts and alleys dominated by a grand royal palace complex.

Until World War II, the country had a proud history of independence, but it was not able to resist the Japanese invasion of 1940. After Japan's defeat, Thailand regained its independence. But now there was the threat of communism, made imminent by the victory of Mao Tse-tung in China in 1949. The communist threat caught the attention of the United States. In 1952, under the newly elected Eisenhower Administration, the US Foreign Service dramatically expanded its operations in Thailand.

A core component of the US commitment was in the area of "information," both in the sense of gathering information about possible threats to the Thai government and in the sense of communicating information to the Thai public about the advantages of the American way of life. The latter mission was squarely in my father's domain. He became a mid-level employee of the United States Information Agency (in Thailand called the United States Information Service, or USIS). He and Genevieve were shipped across the world to accomplish in Thailand what he had done in Germany.

They arrived during a monsoon. To Genevieve, the country appeared wild, culturally barren, alien from anything in her arts-infused life experience. My father promised her that they would not stay long if she could not stand living there. But they both came to love their new home.

After settling in, they had three daughters in quick succession: Sumali, Pichitra, and Lawan. Pichitra's and Lawan's ancestral Thai names were bestowed upon them by none other than the young king of Thailand. Thai royalty is revered among the people, so this was a great honor. My father met the king through one of his golfing buddies, the queen's uncle (who was also the doctor who delivered Pichitra and Lawan). Genevieve met the queen in a special way, through the queen's daughter. Dedicated to ballet, Genevieve was determined to find a way to keep her dance career alive even while living far away from European ballet troupes. Her solution was to start a ballet school. Due to her talents and rigorous teaching approach, the school's reputation spread. The queen, a ballet fan, became aware of it and enrolled her daughter and soon became friendly with Genevieve and my father. The king endowed Genevieve with a royal title (*khunying*), extremely rare for a non-Thai.

My father's relationship with the king aided his diplomatic work. In Thailand, my father worked to open libraries, produce and broadcast radio programs, arrange photography and art exhibits, and put on showings of movies with pro-American messages. He never held a leadership position. Although he was intelligent and competent at what he did, my father was not ambitious. He took things easy. He was content to remain a mid-level official and have time for golf.

My father's supervisors looked askance at his golfing outings during office time. This is where the king saved the day by introducing my father to the entire cadre of government leaders, from the prime minister on down. They all wanted to play golf with this skilled young American golfer who delighted them with his dazzling shots and gave them lessons on the spot. In the words of Lawan, this made my father "untouchable," and his office left him alone as he roamed the links with the Thai leadership. What the office got in return was special attention from Thai officials for the American missions in Thailand. This resulted in invitations to cultural events and official functions that provided the Americans with an improved sense of current Thai sentiments. On the golf course, my father became an informal liaison between the embassy and the palace.

As any golfer knows, an eighteen-hole round leaves lots of spare time for conversation. Lawan remembers my father telling her that the golf course was the place "where a lot of real diplomacy got done." In this way, my father proved his value to his initially skeptical higher-ups. As a rule, USIS officials in Thailand generally were given a single, nonrenewable four-year appointment and then recalled to DC. But my father's initial four-year appointment was renewed one time for another four years and once again for another two, making his posting ten years in all, a record by far, according to Lawan.

Lawan, Sumali, Genevieve, and Iza all mentioned to me that the king loved my father's sense of humor. Biographies of Thailand's recently departed King Bhumibol Adulyadej note that he was a highly respected leader who famously carried himself with a somber visage. One of the authoritative biographies of the king is titled *The King Never Smiles.* I went to the internet for another search, this one guided by my father's name paired with the king's, and found this jewel of a comment on the social network site Medium: "Phil Damon, who worked for USIS, and who was a close personal friend of the King, and often played chess with him, was the first person to make the King smile. Perhaps that is why the

King took care of all his medical needs until he died due to complications with MS. Damon's wife was a close friend of the Queen."

How much of this is fact and how much is exaggeration or legend, I cannot say. I am no professional historian and have exhausted all the sources I have been able to uncover in my amateur family history search. History is also something of a construction, even if done with expertise and boundless resources (in the same way that memory, our own personal history, is always in part constructed). Everyone who knew my father testified to his fun-loving ways and delightfully irreverent sense of humor. To the extent that he really was able to brighten the days of this beloved king, so much the better. That the king and queen took care of my father and his family when they most needed it is beyond question.

My father's working Thai years came to an end in 1964, when he was finally transferred back to the central State Department offices near Washington, DC. I know only two things about his brief stint in the State Department's home office—the two to three years before he was struck with MS, the same terrible disease that felled his own father fifteen years before. The two things I know contributed to my dawning realization that my father was a man of moral purpose. This was a product of my life review that had special meaning for me, since, as I discuss below, it directly connects with my own professional purpose.

The first thing was a comment Lawan heard our father make about his frustration with his fellow State Department employees. "They need to get out and see the countries they're working on." He complained that many State Department officials spent too much time in their offices and too little time on the road. The officials would make pronouncements about countries whose cultures they knew little about. State Department decisions, my father believed, were often flawed due to this lack of firsthand understanding of many foreign countries. These comments certainly sound consistent with the sense I've gained of the man: both his rebelliousness and his outgoing, eager familiarity with people and places he got to know shine through.

The second thing I know about my father's time in DC relates to a side trip he took to Atlanta in April 1968. This trip is lodged in the memory of Sumali, his older daughter, because she accompanied him with Genevieve and Lawan. The trip is also lodged in Sumali's memory because of the momentously tragic occasion that spawned it, Martin Luther King's death. Two weeks after Dr. King's death, my father made the visit to offer his condolences to Coretta Scott King. He wrote ahead to Mrs. King to ask for the visit and arranged the trip to coincide with treatments for his MS in Warm Springs, Georgia. He had never met Mrs. King, but she received him warmly and spent over an hour talking with him while the children played upstairs. Sumali knows nothing about what our father discussed with Mrs. King, but she clearly recalls that "our father idolized MLK Jr." and that he felt deeply bereaved on behalf of Mrs. King. Sumali's account of my father on this occasion moved me. His spontaneous outreach to Mrs. King was entirely in character. It was also in accord with his compassionate concern for mistreated GIs, some of whom were African American, during his Lichfield Trials days.

By the end of the 1960s, my father's MS had taken its toll. Sumali said that at first he thought he had shingles. He became very afraid, then very depressed, when he learned it was the same disease that had taken his father's life. In 1970, he and Genevieve were told that he had less than two years to live.

Then the call came from the secretary to Thailand's queen, who had heard of my father's illness through diplomatic channels. "You must come home now," the secretary told Genevieve on behalf of the queen.

This was my father's last, best shot. He was getting steadily worse in DC, and he could not afford the extensive help needed to carry him around in his semiparalyzed state. A military hospital plane carried my father and his family back to Thailand in 1970. It was the height of the Vietnam War, and the plane had been used to ship wounded GIs home. Since it was returning to Southeast Asia empty, it was available for government passengers who needed to go that way.

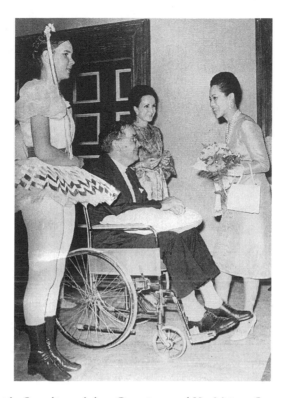

Left to right: Sumali, my father, Genevieve, and Her Majesty Queen Sirikit

When the family reached Bangkok, the king and queen checked my father in to the royal Chulalongkorn hospital with day and night nurses. He lived for another twenty years, defying the predictions of his US doctors. But he did not get better, as he hoped he would once he got back to Thailand. Kenneth MacCormac, my father's colleague in USIA, described seeing my father during one of MacCormac's trips to Bangkok in the 1980s: "He's totally bedridden. I think he's nearly blind. His only source of happiness is the books on records which he gets from the Library of Congress." MacCormac conveyed this account for his 1989 oral history of the USIA, which was then in the process of disbanding. USIA closed down later that year, and most of its records have been thrown away. My father died in 1991.

A Career Woman's Path to Purpose

What about my mother? Left alone after the war, with a young son and the dawning realization that her husband had no intention of returning, what path did her life take?

My mother's most significant spiritual response to her abandonment was to become a devout Roman Catholic. This occurred when I was five. I remember it well; she arranged to have me baptized at the time as well. Faith is a transcendent matter between a person and the higher power the person venerates. It is beyond my capacities for any psychological analysis. I will not speculate here on the cause of my mother's conversion nor on the subsequent journeys, for her or me, of our religious faith. But I will note the uncontestable fact that my father's refusal to come home provided an emotional impetus that paved the way for my mother's spiritual quest.

The Catholic Church became a source of joy, solace, and community for my mother for the remainder of her life. As such, it was a saving compensation for the pain she suffered as an abandoned wife and mother. It is one further example of how people can forge strengths from setbacks by actively seeking ways to positively adapt to misfortunes.

Spiritual growth, no matter how fulfilling, does not pay the bills. My mother needed to find a way to make a living. The 1950s was not an era that welcomed women in the workplace in any kind of professional role. Yet, much like women today, my mother was determined to find a career that would provide her with the financial means she needed to support herself and me and also recognize her talents and interests.

She had little going for her in the way of college education or family connections, but she had smarts, determination, and a genuine love of art and fashion. This cluster of qualities led her to the advertising business, which was picking up steam in the new age of TV and mass media. She learned the rudiments of advertising while volunteering for a local Catholic hospital's public relations department. Before long, she gained the skills and confidence to apply for a real job at Marvin and Leonard, Boston's premier ad agency at the time.

This was the *Mad Men* era. Advertising was a male-dominated industry populated by brash, hard-drinking men who had no sense that women should be treated as equals. My mother was paid poorly for her efforts. As a consequence, we lived humbly, in a run-down apartment on a noisy street. It brings me pain when I think of my mother's financial condition in those years. I'll never forget the day when someone told her about a tiny house for sale in a nearby, low-income neighborhood. She took me to see it with a hopeful spring in her step, then came away with tears in her eyes when she found out that the house was beyond her means. Although I was only ten years old at the time, I still remember the unreachable price tag: $4,000. I am sure that, for my mother, the bitterness of that moment was compounded by the unfairness of her salary. She was as talented and hardworking as many of the men who took home several times as much pay, and she knew it.

But, salary injustice aside, my mother's advertising days were a success. She gained the respect of her male colleagues and earned a reputation as a creative producer and a valuable team member. She was tough and not shy, and eventually she learned to fit well in the highly assertive culture of the advertising industry. The reputation she earned in this first job made it possible for her soon to expand her career in the fashion industry.

By the 1960s, my mother had had enough of the advertising world. She turned her efforts to a more directly creative occupation, designing shoes. In this way she combined her legacy as a child of "shoe city" Brockton with her interest in fashion design. She did well at first, refining the shapes of dress shoes and loafers, and she came into her own as the 1960s progressed into its mod fashion phase. She designed young women's shoes adorned with glitter, lace, and colorful plastic balls. Trendy boutiques in places such as Cambridge, where I was in college, sold her shoes; once I was amused to see a girl I was dating wearing a

My fashionable mother in the 1960s

pair. My mother was successful enough in this trade to become financially comfortable, at least in a modest way. With me away at school and college, she was relieved of providing for anyone but herself; she was able to fully live in accord with her disposition of fierce independence.

In the 1970s, my mother made a move that would define the rest of her life. She picked up her Massachusetts roots and transplanted herself northward, to the state of Maine. It was the first time since her post-high-school sojourn in New York City that she lived anywhere outside a thirty-mile radius of where she was born. As was her way, she made the move alone. But she did not choose Maine randomly. She was inspired by a man she had been reading about but had yet to meet: John Cole, founder and editor of the *Maine Times*, a lively weekly newspaper in the style of the many "underground" papers that grew up in the 1960s.

Cole was an environmentalist and community leader in the college town of Brunswick. My mother took trips there, met Cole, and decided that this was the place where she wanted to spend her remaining years. I knew about this only after she had packed her bags to go.

She bought a modest but charming house near an ocean inlet and set up a small business that enabled her to expand her work beyond designing shoes to creating articles of clothing such as socks, hats, and scarves. She contracted with local groups of lady knitters who turned her designs into well-crafted woolens and called the company "Collab," in reference to her collaboration with these French Canadian crafts-women. The company sold clothes at famous outlets such as L.L. Bean. The woolen clothes she designed had a distinct look, feel, and smell because of their high natural lanolin content. I still have a sweater that she gave me for wearing in the New England winters. The sweater is warm. It's also heavy, stiff, and bulky. It was great for the bitter January winds in New England. I have yet to find use for it in California, but I pull it out from time to time as one would an artsy relic.

My mother truly became herself during her years in Maine. She designed exactly the clothing that fit her aesthetic and lifestyle vision. She made friends with like-minded people her age such as John Cole, and she joined a Catholic community where she found young priests to argue with and, she would admit, to learn from. She hosted me and my three children with verve for countless summer visits, energetically show-ing us the sparkling local sights, such as Winslow Homer's seaside stu-dio. As she found her proper place in Maine, she found herself. In Erikson's phrase, she became a model of ego integrity. She modeled posi-tivity and affirmation for me and my children. We fondly recall her energetic refrain whenever she would make a plan on one of our Maine visits: "Now we're cooking with gas!"

None of this would have happened if my mother's marriage to my father had lasted. It is hard to imagine her having any career at all as a 1950s American wife of a diplomat, let alone the creative fulfillment that her absorbing work in advertising and fashion gave her. As a stay-at-home wife and mother, she would have experienced other joys, but these would have been a world apart from the purposes she found in the life she actually had. What's more, the alternative world of the stable marriage she didn't have might not have been joyful at all. Knowing her, and knowing what I now do about my father, my guess is that their marriage would have come apart quickly, leaving many casualties, including me.

My mother's path to purpose is a story of compensation. The loss of a marriage led directly to the founding of a career that provided her with lifelong satisfaction, and increasingly so as she developed it in a direction that matched her values and her vision. With her friends, her family (me and my children), and her faith, she found enduring personal satisfaction. I can't say for sure that she saw it exactly this way, because I never seized the opportunity to have the right conversations with her while she was still alive. That stands as one of my regrets. But now, acting as her proxy for a life-review reflection, I'll surmise that the meaningful compensations she found after her divorce enabled her to acquire the spirit of affirmation that marks a mature identity and a fulfilled life. My belief is that if my mother had done a life review on her own, it would have concluded with this recognition.

A Path to Purpose in Developmental Psychology

And what of me while my father and mother were making their separate ways in the world? How did their paths to purpose interact with, and affect, my own?

My father's journey after I was born had no direct effects on mine because he adamantly refused to have anything to do with me. This was a conscious decision, as the discovery quest of my life review confirmed: my Thai sisters made it clear that he did not want to discuss me or my existence even by his mid-adulthood years. Consequently, the only way my father influenced me in his postwar period was by not being there. I grew up as one of the world's legions of fatherless children.

In my professional field of developmental psychology, there has been a lot written about the effects of fatherlessness. Some of the findings suggest adverse consequences, such as lower popularity and less satisfying social relationships for fatherless boys. Other findings suggest no differences, at least in some areas of development: fatherless children show no cognitive lags in comparison with other children. Some findings suggest benefits for fatherless children, such as tendencies to be creative and highly productive. Of course I am biased, as is my memory, but I can't recall any special problems with popularity or social relationships other than a succession of awkward moments during adolescence much like most young people encounter. It's true that I never showed cognitive lags, and I suppose my career can be described as creative and productive. But none of these findings reveals a telling insight to me.

For the purposes of my life review, I take such findings under advisement. They convey general population trends. As such, they suggest tendencies that might apply to me, and it might prove informative to be aware of that possibility. But there is always a good amount of variance in any reported population trends. They do not describe every individual. Like everyone else in this world, I am a complex individual with many other things going on in my life apart from my relationship (or non-relationship) with my father. Consequently, I am not destined to be affected by any particular trend found in the general population.

As I noted in chapter 2, a life review is an *individual* enterprise. It can detect patterns in a person's life that explain that one life. Such patterns may, or may not, reflect general trends in the population at large. This is why I noted the distinction between *nomothetic* and *idiographic* study. Nomothetic study looks for normative findings that will level differences among people. Idiographic study looks for findings that can illuminate a particular case in all its uniqueness. The two types of study inform each other, but they do not serve the same purposes. A life review lies squarely in the idiographic study domain because its purpose is to understand the life of one individual.

Beyond the possible, but by no means certain, effects on me of general trends related to fatherlessness, there were particular effects that I noted with more confidence during my life review. Not having a father gave me freedom to explore my own interests without constraining cautions or pressing guidance from a supervising father. I did not need to clear my choice of avocations, friends, living arrangements, or career with anyone. Of course I also received no fatherly help in any of these matters, and I sometimes stumbled and made some misguided choices that I needed to correct. But doing this on my own had some salutary outcomes. Learning to fend for myself without the guiding hand of a father enhanced my sense of independence and also gave me a chance to develop skills and strengths I may not have achieved if I hadn't needed to do so. (The contrasting example of my father's school-days insouciance, revealed by life review, supports this realization.) Further, my ambition, which I consider a healthy characteristic when kept within proper limits, was fostered by the dodgy economic situation my father's absence left us in. These all were indirect effects that my father's absence had on me, influences that I did not notice at the time but that emerged in my consciousness while doing my life review. My awareness of these effects augmented the huge revelation I discussed in chapter 4: the life-transforming effect of my father's attending the same school that my mother sent me to twenty-two years after he'd been a student there.

In contrast to my father's postwar journey, my mother's affected me directly in countless ways. In my life review, I identified several that seemed especially important in ways I had not fully appreciated before. As I contemplated the trajectory of my mother's work life, it occurred to me that she presented a model of purposeful productivity that, over time, increasingly reflected her special talents and vision. She needed to earn a living and always worked within the system to do that, and over the years she found ways to tailor her work life to her own creative instincts. I have no memory of being consciously influenced by the model she set, but looking back, I feel comfortable in speculating that it must have rubbed off on me. Also, of course, she operated as a woman at a time before this was easily done or well accepted in men's fields such as advertising. Not only did her example predispose me to accept the importance of gender equality; it also showed me firsthand how someone with determination and grit can level the playing field against daunting odds.

The other realization regarding my mother's influence that arose from my life review was the importance to me of her conversion to the Catholic faith. My own spiritual journey should be of no interest to anyone but me, and I have no ability to write about matters of religious doctrine. But I can say that faith has been an important part of my life and that my work on purpose and moral commitment reflects a continuing interest that I trace back to my early religious education. My research and writings have never been doctrinal, but I have written about religious concepts such as the Golden Rule (some versions of which can be found in every major religion). I have written about the value of religious faith for youth development, again from a nondenominational perspective. This work has gone against the grain of my field. In contemporary academic social science, interests in religious faith have been unusual and even discouraged at times. In the late 1990s, when I became editor of *The Handbook of Child Development*, one of the field's major establishment sources, I commissioned a chapter on faith development. That was a first for that venue, and I met resistance from colleagues who doubted there was sufficient good work on this topic to merit a chapter in such an esteemed outlet. I attribute my personal and professional interests in faith to the commitments my mother fostered in me as part of her own faith journey. My willingness to go against the grain of my profession in this regard may also owe a debt to the model of determined independence that my mother offered me.

In conducting my life review, I found it informative to trace my intellectual development as it advanced my unfolding purposes. The purpose I found in discovering and communicating new findings while writing for my high school paper turned into my lifelong vocational purpose. I've pursued it in the forms of lecturing, studying human development, writing for professional and public audiences, and communicating through internet outlets such as YouTube, podcasts, and websites. This is a vocation of knowledge and understanding, and consequently my vocational path has been guided by the course of my intellectual development.

Accordingly, here I relate my intellectual history during the period when my father and mother were making their way in what we academics call "the real world." I am well aware that my story has little of the drama, color, or faraway romance that characterized my father's path, nor have I encountered the kinds of barriers that my mother went up against and broke through as a career woman in the 1950s. Still, my vocational path has been deeply engaging, at least for me. I know many who share my interest in the intellectual history of developmental psychology, the field that I've contributed to, so herewith is an account of my interactions with that history.

My choice of psychology as my primary research field came about in the summer after high school. Someone placed in my hands a copy of a book of selected papers by Edwin Boring called *History, Psychology, and Science*. I do not recall anything specific from the book, but I do remember finding the mix of fields indicated by the title fascinating and compelling, and I liked the way Boring combined rigor with conceptual breadth. I determined at that point to become the same type of psychologist.

After high school, the timing of my undergraduate study was fortunate: my college years at Harvard overlapped with its short-lived Department of Social Relations, which was set up to encourage cross-disciplinary exploration in the social sciences. Students had access to brilliant scholars from a range of disciplines, particularly anthropology, sociology, and psychology. My sophomore tutor was the esteemed sociologist Talcott Parsons, my senior thesis adviser was the great social psychologist Roger Brown, and I attended courses and lectures by legendary scholars such as Gordon Allport, Henry Murray, Erik Erikson, Stanley Milgram, and David Riesman. My introduction to child development was a spellbinding course by Jerome Kagan. My introduction to cognitive science was Jerome Bruner's course in perception and cognition. It was an incredibly stimulating environment for broad social-science learning. I came away with an appreciation of distinct conceptual frameworks and diverse methods of inquiry.

In keeping with the personality traits my life review highlighted, I did not always behave myself in the company of these distinguished academic mentors. I wrote a senior honors thesis about whether children could infer emotions from the actions of heroes in Homer's *Iliad*. It was an early version of "qualitative" research (not well regarded at the time), and my approach was to describe ways of thinking that enabled some children to understand the link between actions and emotions correctly. When I presented the thesis to the reviewing faculty committee, Jerome Kagan told me that when analyzing the ways of thinking that I described, I should control for the number of words the children used in their responses. Rather than listen and learn from what this celebrated child psychologist had to say, I responded with outrage and refused to implement the statistical control he suggested. My point was that the number of words of course would co-vary with the ways of thinking, since the more complex ways take more words to explain, but this tells us nothing because it's the ways of thinking that drive the word use rather than the other way around. I still believe I was right on this point, but my behavior was wholly inappropriate for a young student receiving feedback from one of the leaders in the field. The comment from my dorm master at Andover, uncovered through my life review, brought home to me how much such behavior was in character during my youth: "He prides himself on being broad-minded and liberal, but he is apt to be stubborn and get no further than his own point of view." It also has renewed my determination to watch out for this endemic stubbornness now and in the future.

In addition to renowned senior professors, I met two graduate students who augmented my education in consequential ways. One was Douglas Carmichael, who told me to read Piaget and who also suggested that I apply to his alma mater, the University of California, Berkeley, for doctoral study. The other graduate student I met at this time was Howard Gardner, who has been my lifelong friend and treasured collaborator ever since.

Late in my senior year of college, Roger Brown called me into his office. Roger was not only my thesis adviser but also a role model for how a scholar could conduct careful research with a far-reaching and deeply humane vision. For an illustrious academic star, he was also amazingly considerate and gentle as an adviser to his students. But on this occasion he was not so kind and gentle. Rather, he spoke with a tone of annoyance in his voice that was unique in all my experience with him. He told me the Harvard psychology department's graduate

Graduating college

admissions committee had turned down my application. He asked me, with uncharacteristic irritation, why I had "made such a mess of" my application.

I knew what he was referring to. In my statement of academic purpose, I had concocted a plan to study "developmental sociology," whatever that was (and I certainly did not know). I was imagining using insights from Jean Piaget, Erik Erikson, Erving Goffman, and Talcott Parsons (the people I was reading in those days) to chart the course of human progress toward social harmony and personal fulfillment. My idealistic graduate application statement did not fly, and I was too *stubborn*—that old personality trait—to take Roger up on his gracious offer to let me submit a revised statement for admissions to Harvard. I went away from that meeting peeved at what I perceived to be the narrow-mindedness of Harvard's psychology department, and I told myself that it was time for me to move to greener pastures. Fortunately, Berkeley's psychology department overlooked whatever nonsense I wrote on its application and accepted me anyway, most likely because Roger Brown had written me a good enough recommendation.

Once at Berkeley, I actually did manage to study how social and individual dimensions of life experience come together (or "dynamically interact," in the phraseology of the field) in the course of human development. My permission to work on this complex matter was much to the credit of my professors (Jonas Langer and Paul Mussen), who were not only knowledgeable in their own areas of specialization but also tolerant of a student's desire to integrate and expand areas. Today there is so much known about the dynamic interplay of developmental systems that it is hard to recapture how out of the box this line of research seemed in the early 1970s. I distinctly remember the puzzlement I encountered while seeking a dissertation committee for a subject I was calling "social cognition." To the faculty whom I asked to supervise me, the subject sounded not only unfamiliar but possibly illusory. How quickly things changed: social cognition became a major part of the field soon thereafter and has remained so ever since. One of my early papers as a young scholar was an effort to justify this as a legitimate field of study, an argument that would seem trivial today.

The research I began while a graduate student at Berkeley was aimed at uncovering the previously uncharted depths of social cognition that young people use in their everyday lives. I had some inkling of how socially smart even little-educated adolescents could be from a summer I spent during college as a camp counselor at a day camp for underprivileged youth in Dorchester, Massachusetts, and also from social work I did in the Bronx for a short while after college. For part of my social work in the Bronx, I was assigned to a settlement house where teenagers from the neighborhood were encouraged to hang out so that they would not get into (or cause) trouble. For one activity, I asked them to write and perform skits about people they knew in their communities or people they heard about from the news. As I watched the skits that they produced, I was astonished by how much they knew about the social world around them. Their knowledge of people and events was extensive, and their perceptions and insights were sharp as a tack. From my observations in Dorchester and the Bronx, I could see that even underprivileged young people understood far more about the social world than anything previous psychological research had documented.

At that time in developmental psychology, there were two dominant characterizations of social understanding in childhood and adolescence. The first was a well-known series of studies on "person perception" (the phrase that stood for social cognition in those days). The bottom line of these studies was that, with development, the child's understanding of people moves from the "overt" to the "covert": early on, children think of people in terms of surface qualities such as physical looks, and as they get older, they perceive "inner" traits such as intentions and virtues. The second dominant view came from Kohlberg's moral judgment stage system, which placed the origins of moral cognition in the conception of power and authority that defined his Stage 1. In this view, children begin thinking about the social world as structured around the commands of authority figures such as parents and God, and they make judgments about right and wrong accordingly.

Although I respected both lines of work and learned much about investigatory methods from them, neither view seemed sufficient to me. The person perception studies were limited for two reasons: First, social cognition is mainly thinking about *relations* and *transactions* between people, since these are what we experience firsthand, especially when young. A sole focus on thinking about what other people are like misses this relational view entirely. Second, I suspected that children knew more about the "inner" than they were given credit for, and that older people cared more about the "outer" than existing studies claimed. As for the Kohlberg stage system, it missed the obvious fact that children's playgroups are full of moral behavior such as sharing, compassion, and an insistence on fairness. To say that children's morality simply begins with a "Stage 1" obedience to authority neglects the very real moral sense that even preschool children have.

While exploring children's social cognition, I started the research that led to my first book, *The Social World of The Child*. When the book came out, it brought me unexpected prominence in the field when it was given the lead review in *Contemporary Psychology*, psychology's only book review venue at that time. That experience bonded me to the process of book writing, just as the teenage sports coverage for my school newspaper bonded me to the process of writing about research. Over the next fifteen years, I conducted research that charted the growth of social concepts from childhood through late adolescence. The concepts I investigated included authority, justice, social rules, and self-understanding. I did this research while a faculty member at Clark University in Worcester, Massachusetts, a vigorous beehive of developmental theory at that time. My fifteen years there, starting as an assistant professor, were among the most stimulating of my intellectual life. I still draw on the conceptual capital that I acquired in those days.

At the end of the 1980s, I wound down this first phase of my research career, for several reasons. None of my studies had been able to shed much light on the nature of the link between understanding and actual behavior, which left a large gap in my accounts of social-cognitive development. I had made a bit of progress at the edges of this problem, finding weak associations between children's concepts of justice and their sharing behavior and then examining how peer social interactions can lead to more advanced justice reasoning. But these minor efforts aside, my work had left the mysteries of real-life social conduct mainly unexplored.

I decided to take on these mysteries more directly, turning my focus to people's real-life goals and commitment rather than only their understanding and reasoning. This venture into the stuff of real-world conduct coincided with a major career move that I made in 1989: I left Clark to become chair of the Education Department at Brown University and eventually director of the Center for the Study of Human Development. Under the spectacular leadership of Vartan Gregorian, Brown was a lively place where scholars were given encouragement to expand their horizons.

At around this time, Anne Colby and I received an invitation from the Social Science Research Council (SSRC) to meet with a committee on giftedness that the council had established. The committee wanted to discuss with us whether there was such a thing as moral giftedness and, if so, how it could be defined and studied. Anne and I had been fellow travelers on the moral psychology circuit for a number of years, and we were, not incidentally, also married; we had, however, never done any research together. Neither of us had thought much about the question of moral giftedness. The only paradigm in the field that might be used to address this at the time was Kohlberg's moral judgment stage system, which defined a supreme stage of reasoning (Stage 6) so rare that it was actually omitted from the official Kohlberg stage-scoring manual. Elevated as this stage of reasoning might have been, Anne and I agreed that it was too cognitive in nature to provide a sufficient basis for anything as big-hearted as moral giftedness. For access to this question, we knew we would need to invoke concepts like courage, grit, compassion, and truthfulness, capacities that had been intentionally dismissed in Kohlberg's theory as haphazard components of an unanalyzable "bag of virtues."

After some back-and-forth with the SSRC committee (members of which included David Feldman and Howard Gardner), Anne and I received a $6,000 grant to conduct a study of people we chose to call "moral exemplars" (we worried that the "giftedness" label would give our work in this area a bias toward a biological heredity explanation). We used these funds to conduct a two-year nominating study with twenty distinguished scholars from a range of disciplines and belief traditions. The nominators helped us define criteria and come up with names of living exemplars who met these criteria. On the basis of this lengthy procedure, we contacted potential subjects for the study and eventually found twenty-three exemplars who agreed to participate.

At that point, at David Feldman's suggestion, we found a small foundation in California (the Institute for Noetic Sciences) that agreed to match our SSRC grant through some funds they had received to examine "the altruistic spirit." Thus, with the grand total of $12,000 in grants, we embarked on one of the most fruitful and meaningful efforts that either of us had been fortunate enough to engage in to this point in our professional careers. The initial result of this effort was the book *Some Do Care*, and the consequences of the project have lived on far beyond that, in my later research on "good work," in our recent book on moral formation among extraordinary twentieth-century historical leaders, *The Power of Ideals*, and in the recent upsurge of interest in the exemplar methodology as a crucial research tool for positive psychology.

The research that we published in *Some Do Care* yielded a number of surprises. We had gone into the study expecting to hear these extraordinary individuals—many of whom laid their lives on the line for civil rights, justice, world peace, and other moral causes—tell us about how they manage their fears and sustain their courage. But every one of our subjects denied needing courage for what they did. Their common refrain was that they rarely experienced fear, because they felt that they had no choice other than to do what they knew was right. Such unanimity of response, even in a small sample, suggests that this finding was no anomaly. The responses indicated a degree of moral certainty that preempted normal concerns for personal protection and security.

This unexpected finding led us to look closely at the basis for our exemplars' certainty. Again to our surprise, a very high percentage of the sample (over 90 percent) cited faith in a higher power as the basis for their willingness to forgo personal concerns about security. For those with traditional religious views, it was faith in God's will ("the Lord will provide," was the way one exemplar put it). For others, it was faith in some other form of transcendent spiritual power.

Upon publication, *Some Do Care* was considered a groundbreaking work for its ideas and its "exemplar" methodology, which brought new life to psychology's venerable but out-of-fashion case-study approach. The book continues to be influential to this day. Obviously I was pleased by the success of our book, but beyond that, our study of moral exemplars made a lasting mark on me personally. Time and again, I found myself returning from an interview with an exhilarating sense of inspiration. That feeling and the lessons our exemplars' lives conveyed have stayed with me to this day. Further, that investigation's focus on moral courage primed me for my intense interest in the story I uncovered regarding my father's testimonies at the Lichfield Trials. As I dug through the documents describing his activity as a witness at those trials, I recognized the behavioral patterns we wrote about in *Some Do Care*. In that episode of his life, my father acted out of true moral commitment.

Two years after the publication of *Some Do Care*, I spent a sabbatical year at the Center for Advanced Study in the Behavioral Sciences at Stanford University. During that year, I teamed up with Howard Gardner and Mihaly Csikszentmihalyi to launch the Good Work Project. Our aim was to understand how dedicated professionals manage to conduct work that is both excellent and ethical under conditions of pressure and negative incentives. We wanted to learn how some people succeed in ignoring or rejecting such pressures The Good Work Project examined several vocational fields, such as education, journalism, biological science, and business, and gave birth to cutting-edge books and journal articles. It also led to educational efforts to promote good work among mid-career professionals and among younger people still in school. Under the leadership of Howard Gardner, the project now has expanded to become a broad-based effort to encourage "ethical, excellent, and engaging work" across all of society. Renamed "the Good Project," it is based at Harvard's Graduate School of Education, and it is going strong today.

To me, the most striking finding from our Good Work studies was the clarity and intensity with which dedicated workers from all fields held on to their field's public mission. This finding led me directly into the third phase of my research career, studies in the formation of purpose, the personal equivalent of the mission of a vocational field.

The importance of purpose for a fulfilled life has been recognized in popular writings and spiritual teachings for centuries. I spent some time searching through the wisdom of the ages on the subject of purpose. I found the philosophical and spiritual writings on purpose to be rich and informative. Before settling on my own approach, I digested the highlights of what I had been reading and wrote a short book of sayings and quotes, interspersed with essays that I wrote summarizing what was then known about how purpose functions in human life and how it develops over the life span. The eminent psychologist David Meyers did me the honor of writing an introduction to this little book. I called it *Noble Purpose*. Immediately after that, I launched my research program on how people of all ages find and pursue purpose, beginning in early adolescence and continuing through the entire life span into the "encore" and elderly years.

I determined to examine these philosophical and spiritual speculations in an empirical manner. Despite the ages-old recognition of the central role of purpose in a well-directed life, the construct had been given surprisingly little attention in scientific study. There had been some interest in "meaning," but meaning, although important and related to purpose, is not the same thing. Meaning is a broad concept that includes anything that people consider to be personally significant. Purpose in part relies on meaning (if something is nonmeaningful to the self, it will not trigger a sense of purpose), but purpose also implies an intention to accomplish something beyond the self. There has also been some important work on resilience. But even though it is true that resilience is a beneficial outcome of purpose, it is not purpose's only psychological benefit. Here I had been influenced by my participation in two intellectual movements that had recently captured the imagination of many psychologists: positive psychology, introduced by Martin Seligman and Mihaly Csikszentmihalyi, and positive youth development, for which Peter Benson, Richard Lerner, and I had been early advocates. Both movements urged an increased focus on people's strengths and "assets." The two movements shared a sense that the scientific view of human behavior had been distorted by an overemphasis on problems, neuroses, conflicts, and other "deficits."

As one personal illustration of this, I remember the first day I entered the building that housed the Stanford Center on Adolescence. The walls of the corridor were lined with posters announcing the dread statistics on youth misbehavior: soaring rates of homicide, suicide, violence, drug use, and so on. After walking this gauntlet, one could not help feeling that young people today are little more than objects of concern and worry for our society, problems to be dealt with rather than bright sources of contributions. When I assumed the center's directorship in fall 1997, my first act was to remove those posters.

Looking back, in life-review fashion, at the choices I made to determine the direction of my work, my change in focus from social cognition to real-life moral commitment and purpose is an important part of the story, but not the only one. The other part is the choice I made, early in my career, to do problem-centered research rather than attempt theory-building. This was not a common choice for an ambitious scholar at that time. When I was in graduate school, I was often told by my men-tors that the pinnacle of achievement in the social sciences was to cre-ate a theoretical model that would leave a mark on the field. Grand theo-ries were the order of the day. They were esteemed and vigorously discussed. In psychology, attention was riveted on the distinctions between the theories of Freud, Skinner, Piaget, Vygotsky, Simon, and a host of theoretical-model builders who followed in their wake. To do basic research in service of creating, improving, or even rejecting one of the field's grand theories was considered the highest intellectual calling possible.

Raising the stakes were the ideological messages that scholars at that time read into the contending grand theories. Theoretical discus-sions often led to intense ideological debates. Theories were considered to be entire worldviews that determined everything from the judg-ments that people make to the values they live by. The tenor of the argument could reach a fevered pitch. For example, during the Paris student revolts of the Vietnam War era, Howard Gardner made the following observation about the theoretical position known as structuralism:

> The uprising of 1968 signaled a new shift in intellectual allegiance among the students. . . . "Structuralism is dead" cried the students. Whether or not they had ever read a word of Piaget or Levi-Strauss, they sensed a tie between the philosophy of these men and the estab-lishment they had come to despise.

Even in scholarly journals, assumptions were fiercely contested, and abstract academic rhetoric took on an air that veered toward the apoca-lyptic. For example, just as I was finishing graduate school, I came across a critique of Kohlberg's moral development theory that amazed me. This early statement of a cultural perspective, published in the touchstone journal *Human Development*, concluded in the following manner:

The moral reasoning which we see actively applied today by the Western world, quite apart from high-minded professional philosophy, bids fair to destroy man. . . . We would do better to explore and analyze differences wherever found, to borrow and adapt, and to nurture invention and cultural mutation as it occurs, than to perpetuate the ideology of a suicidal world trying to reconcile its differences through the use of a theoretical framework ill-suited for containing and ordering real human diversity.

This was really taking psychological theory seriously. The author was proposing that Kohlberg had devalued the perspectives of people living in non-Western cultures by claiming universality for a stage sequence that had been founded on Western philosophical assumptions and empirically validated by research with Western subjects. This raised, in the author's mind, the danger of a theoretical imperialism that could lead to cultural conflict and, ultimately, to world destruction. Nowadays, proposing a link between an academic theory of moral judgment and the destruction of humankind may seem a bit hyperbolic, but at that time it almost sounded like a reasonable conjecture.

In some ways, such a concern with the big picture of ideology and theory had been a welcome change for American psychology, which was just emerging from a decades-long bout of what had been derided as "dust-bowl empiricism." The field of child development was now moving past the lifeless agenda of simply cataloging skills and behaviors of children at various phases of their growth trajectories or of recording "a day in the life of the child" from dawn to dusk. The theoretical debates of the 1960s and 1970s brought excitement and drama to the field and added value to the research that scholars were choosing to do.

But theoretic discourse has its limitations too, especially if it becomes detached from the problems and data that the theories are intended to explain. The developmental literature of the 1970s was full of nuanced discussions contrasting universalism and contextualism, or comparing Piaget with Vygotsky or behaviorism with cognitive science, or making the cases for biological, environmental, and/or interactionist explanations of behavior. But it was hard to use the insights generated by these discussions to answer common questions such as: How should a parent or teacher deal with a difficult child? How does TV (or the then-new computer or video games) affect learning during childhood and adolescence? What kinds of friendships do youngsters benefit most from? Why do many youngsters gravitate toward antisocial and destructive behavior? Where do adolescents find the goals and motives that shape their life choices? What variations in family patterns across time and social context influence the perspectives of the young? Do young people today have different challenges from those faced by children of previous generations? These are the kinds of questions that people outside our field seek answers to. It seemed to me that a more problem-centered and less theoretically driven type of research was needed to address such questions. I was by no means the only scholar at that time who made this observation. In 1975, my old mentor Roger Brown announced in a textbook he cowrote that "the days of the grand theory are over."

What's more, the use of psychological theory to contest highly charged social and political ideology seemed to me incommensurate with the goals of open-minded scientific inquiry, on the one hand; but on the other hand, nor could a return to sterile empiricism serve a constructive purpose. I always believed that ideology should be avoided in science; yet ideas must be put front and center, even when the goal is to promote practical solutions to problems. What seemed apparent to me at the time was that the profound conceptual work that had gone into building and critiquing developmental theories could be mined for its potential to help us understand the common problems of human development.

For my own work, I decided to go with problems of interest that could be addressed by an approach informed by available conceptual distinctions but not bound to any one theoretical or ideological system. At the same time, I was hoping that grappling with such problems would inform theory-building, so that the benefits of such an enterprise would flow two ways, from theory to problem and back again. This remains my goal. As such, my research has grown out of the intellectual climate of our times, although it is also true that I have conducted it in my own way.

To keep myself attuned to the range of new ideas emerging from developmental science, I also took on another absorbing scholarly activity, editing collections of other scholars' writings. Two engagements were especially significant: in 1978, I founded the series *New Directions for Child and Adolescent Development*, which I continued editing for the next twenty-five years; and in 1998, I became editor in chief of *The Handbook of Child Psychology: The Fifth Edition* and, in 2006, coeditor, with Richard Lerner, of the sixth edition. The *New Directions* series proved to be one of the great learning experiences of my life. During my editorship, the series opened up new approaches to many areas of the field, giving me at least a passing acquaintance with an enormous range of topics. Based on my work with that series, I was offered the editorship of *The Handbook of Child Psychology*, which had been the landmark organizer of research in our field for over sixty years. With an extremely talented and dedicated group of coeditors (Richard Lerner, Robert Siegler, Deanna Kuhn, Nancy Eisenberg, Irving Sigel, and Anne Renninger), we produced a four-volume set that gave the handbook's grand tradition a forward-looking treatment similar to the New Directions series.

The other absorbing scholarly activity that has accompanied my research career is the writing of trade books aimed at a general audience. I did not come up with this idea on my own. In the mid-1980s, a young editor from the Free Press who had heard me speak about moral development asked me whether I would be interested in writing a short book on what was known in this area. It so happened that I had a draft manuscript on this subject that I had been unsuccessfully trying to sell to Harvard University Press. I revised the entire thing (always a useful move whenever possible) and sent it to the Free Press, which put it out as *The Moral Child*. Much to my surprise, the book found a sizable readership, which included not just university faculty and students but also parents and other members of the public (somehow even getting a mention in *Vogue* magazine, of all unexpected places). This experience whetted my appetite for popular writing. In the mid-1990s, I published *Greater Expectations*, which landed me on dozens of national media shows, including *The Oprah Winfrey Show* (to my bewilderment and near panic). That book made the case for raising young people with high standards for achievement and service. Nowadays this message sounds almost banal, but the 1990s were the heyday of the self-esteem movement, and in that overindulgent climate, my book went enough against the grain to attract attention and controversy. *Greater Expectations* went through several printings and remains my best-selling book. There is no way to know its contribution to public opinion, but I do believe that the ideas and practices that it criticized have been on the wane since I wrote it. A follow-up book proposing a community-based strategy for raising young people with high standards was met with less interest. I was told by my publicist that this was because readers gravitate more to social criticism than to accounts of possible solutions. If so, this seems to me an unfortunate disposition for the purpose of constructive problem-solving. The strategy that I proposed in that follow-up book (a "youth charter" of high standards that each community would work out in conversations between adults and young people) received some attention, and a few places tried it out, with some success. But the strategy proved too labor-intensive for broad application. It also became too time-consuming for my own schedule after I relocated to Stanford, so I regretfully let this promising initiative drop. At Stanford, I began my research program on the development of purpose, which eventually led to *The Path to Purpose* and the multitude of studies that my many extraordinary students have done to expand our understanding of purpose beyond anything I could have imagined on my own.

Unlike my mother's and father's stories, mine is still ongoing. My work to date has taken the directions I've described. I haven't stopped trying out new directions, including the one I am taking with this book. It is too early to review the results of this direction, so I shall leave it there, waiting to see if any of the spaghetti sticks to the wall, as my college roommate Alessandro Vitelli taught me to say.

7

A Round of Golf with My Father

"**PHIL WAS A** big, outgoing guy, a great golfer . . ."

When I read those words in Kenneth MacCormac's USIA oral history, the first document I found in my quest to learn about my father, a mix of delight and frustration swept over me. Delight at the thought of my father mastering the infinitely challenging game of golf. Frustration at realizing that I never had a chance to play the game with him.

Several years and hundreds of documents later, I have found out much more about my father. I have many reasons to regret never knowing him. Yet among all that I've uncovered, there is nothing that has had quite the same sting as my discovery of his golfing prowess when I first read the MacCormac transcript.

As soon as I stumbled upon the game of golf at around age ten, it was love at first swing. But I had to learn how to play on my own. I couldn't afford lessons and had no father around to give me advice. When I finally discovered that my father was expert at the game, my sorrow over never having had a chance to play with him was not a sweet one. Couldn't he have shown up just once to show me how to play the game? If ever

I allowed myself to feel resentment about my father's absence, it was located exactly there.

Reports of my father's golf game sprang up all along my road to discovery. When I first met Aunt Verna, she mentioned that he saw his golf skill as "something he was quite proud of." My sister Lawan added further material to Verna's account, recalling that our father maintained a low single-digit handicap throughout his playing days. His grandson Albert noted that my father earned a spot on the wall at his golf club, the venerable Royal Club in Bangkok, with a great tournament victory. Sumali confirmed my conjecture that my father's golf game helped his diplomatic career in Thailand because high-level Thai government officials enjoyed playing with him.

There were many basic life skills that I needed to figure out without a father to help me, all of which were far more practical than golf. Yet among all the ways that my father wasn't there to guide my growing up, the one that most keenly bothered me was his absence on the golf course. Perhaps this was because the game meant a lot to him, and to me—something that was special for both of us that we could have shared. Perhaps it was because in most areas of my life I was able to do pretty well without his help. Golf is one exasperating exception: my inconsistent game never soars beyond occasional flashes of glory. For whatever reason, my father's absence in this area gnawed at me when I first encountered it, and it rankles to this day.

But sometimes, with luck and longevity, life has a way of filling in some of the missing pieces. I finally did manage to get a "distance learning" golf lesson from my father after all these years. The occasion was my first visit with Iza Warner, which took place in 2015 when she was a youthful ninety-two.

Iza's immediate graciousness to me on that first visit bore two memorable fruits. The first was a kindhearted exclamation. In the midst of that initial meeting, out of the blue, Iza looked at me and remarked, "You father would have liked you." Although this seemed a modest enough compliment, it proved powerful in its impact on me. It was something I must have longed to hear, even in my mid-sixties.

Iza's second gift came the week after our meeting. Back home, I received from her a small assortment of timeworn black-and-white photos of my father in the 1950s soon after he arrived in Thailand. Among them was a picture of him on a Thai golf course, dressed in white colonial garb and surrounded by young Thai caddies. My father was caught in motion taking a full swing at the ball with his wedge club. He had just completed his chip shot, a spray of grass and dirt still hanging in the air.

It was my father's pose that struck me. He was looking down at where the ball *had been* before he smacked it. If you are a golfer, you must know how hard this is to do—and also how important it is to do. The temptation is to follow the ball's flight with your eyes to see whether or not you made a decent shot—and to find out whether or not the golf gods have given you a good bounce. Keeping your head down *past the strike* is a way to increase the odds of a good shot, but it's much easier said than done. It requires concentration, good habits, discipline, focus, and self-control, all the virtues called for by this most demanding game.

Looking at the photo Iza had sent, I had before me a vivid example of highly skilled golfing behavior performed by my very own father. *This was the one and only lesson I would ever get from him.* That lesson took. Ever since I implanted that picture in my mind, I've rarely looked up during a chip shot. My handicap has come down two strokes since then. I like to think those strokes can be attributed to the photographic lesson my father gave me across a half century.

The Meaning of Golf

In my life, golf has meant many things, including but not restricted to the weekend sport that so many people enjoy as a pleasant pastime. I started playing as a preteen on a scruffy muni course in my down-at-the-heels hometown, far from the manicured world of country-club golf. A phys ed instructor at my junior high offered his students passes to the local muni course at fifty cents a pop. Even in the late 1950s, this was a bargain. I found a friend who also saw the appeal of this, and we'd rush out after school and squeeze in twenty-seven holes of fast-paced play before we had to be home for dinner.

I have no record of how I played in those days, but I distinctly recall loving everything about it: the expansive feeling of escaping the confines of home and school for a roam through a parklike environment; the power of sending a little white ball soaring hundreds of yards with a single strike; the sportsmanlike way that golfers root for the success of fellow players even while competing against them; the inane, obsessive rules of the sport; and the thrilling way that playing a hole can turn from triumph to disaster and then back again without warning.

Actually I do have one memory of a golf result of sorts that I achieved in my preteen days. It was not a score on a round of golf; it was, rather, a performance on a driving contest at a summer camp I attended at age twelve. My memory of that event is vivid, probably because I did so well. We contestants all lined up to peform our drives, and then lined up once again for a second chance. My first drive went long and straight, way past all the others. Then, minutes later, to the sound of admiring gasps, my second drive soared twenty yards past my first one (which still stood as the longest drive by far). I took home a camp trophy for that feat, a concrete reminder that this glorious event actually did happen.

Yet there is an odd twist to this story, one that illustrates the unreliable nature of memory that I've written about in chapter 1. More than fifty years after that driving contest, I attended a reunion for the now well-aged former attendees of that summer camp. Few people at the reunion knew or recognized me: unlike school classmates, fellow campers do not tend to form lifelong bonds with one another. But one friendly fellow did light up when he saw me. He was a couple of years younger than me, and we did not know each other well when we were at camp together. But he recalled my driving contest victory.

"I remember what happened. Everyone was talking about it that summer," he said, practically jumping up and down as he spoke. "Billy Damon hit a golf ball 250 yards with a putter!" Well—of course this was wrong: *I used a driver*, like everyone else. But try as I might, I could not get the fellow to remove the putter part of the story from his memory. It was sealed in place, an integral part of his recollection. He was 100 percent sure that it happened that way. I note this encounter here to further illustrate the constructed nature of recollections, as I discussed in chapter 1. My guess is that my campmate's memory unintentionally added this twist to somehow distinguish the true exceptionality of my feat, which was that I drove *both*, not just one, of my shots far beyond anyone else's two attempts, although I certainly did not use a putter to do this.

After junior high, I gave up golfing for forty years, replacing it with the more responsible goals of raising three children and managing a career. This really is the main reason why my golf handicap hovers around a modest 18; I can't in all fairness blame it on my father. During the forty years of my golfing exile, I made only a few visits to random courses I happened upon. Over that long stretch of time, I saw golf as a forbidden pleasure, a time-sink that was hard to defend and maybe even dangerously addictive. My guilt over wasting precious time ruled the day. I kept my guard up and limited myself to sports that took less time and required more running around and sweating, such as tennis and pickup basketball. During the few times I ventured out on golf courses, I was furtive and inept.

One way to get rid of a temptation is to give in to it, to rephrase Oscar Wilde's famous dictum. This can be especially effective once the reasons for resisting the temptation start to fade. After my children left home and settled into their own lives, new time opened up in my life. I reentered the world of golf, tentatively at first, like a returning exile who feels uncomfortable in his native land. My swing came back, for what it's worth, although I discovered to my dismay that in my youth I had self-taught myself a bad grip, and I had to spend months unlearning that. More pleasantly, I reacquainted myself with the game's distinctive customs and culture, a formalized blend of comradery, competition, and courtesy. I find the game to be engrossing and humbling, both of which are beneficial for me. Unlike my father, I am far from a "great golfer." But my uneven play is nevertheless elevated by the "flow" (technically known in psychology as "optimal experience") that I often feel when I'm on a course. As a nod to my lingering sense that I shouldn't be wasting time, I vastly prefer really fast golf.

Playing golf engages four basic human senses. The *physical* is obvious, especially when you eschew an electric golf cart and trudge around the course carrying your clubs. There is also the *social* (players who compete—and bet with—one another while rooting for their fellows in a spirit of sportsmanship); the *mental* (state of mind determines the outcome of every shot); and the *mystical*.

Yes, I said "the mystical." This may sound like a stretch, but I have felt it in peak moments, and it has been lyrically explained in some of the great golf literature, from John Updike's *Golf Dreams* to Michael Murphy's *Golf in the Kingdom*.

Updike's initial contribution to unraveling the mysteries of golf was taxonomic. In an effort to determine exactly what species of activity golf constitutes, Updike considered categories such as hobby, work, play, and sightseeing. He finally settled on a category replete with supersensory, psychedelic connotations: golf, he wrote, is best understood as a *trip*. Here's what he had to say on the matter, in his gloriously florid—and slyly humorous—prose:

A non-chemical hallucinogen, golf breaks the human body into components so strangely elongated and so tenuously linked, yet with
anxious little bunches of hyper-consciousness and . . . a sort of car-
tilaginous euphoria—golf so transforms one's somatic sense, in short,
that truth itself seems to break through the exacerbated and as it
were debunked fabric of mundane reality.

I agree! Indeed, I stand in awe of how well Updike's half-humorous
depiction captures the way a golf swing is greater than the sum of its
parts—seemingly imbued, when it goes right, with a transcendent sense
of body, mind, and place.

More otherworldly still is Michael Murphy's treatment of "the Great
Game" as played in its original home next to Scotland's Firth of Forth.
In his bestselling 1972 book *Golf in the Kingdom* (more than a million
copies sold in nineteen languages), Murphy takes his reader hole-by-
hole along a mystery-cloaked course that he calls "Burningbush." The
players include a savant named Shivas Irons, who offers his young
American companion (a fictional version of Murphy) attitudinal advice
about golf and Zen meditative sport practices that enhance experience as
well as performance. All the ancient holes of Burningbush shimmer
with mysteries and spirits.

The not-so-well-kept secret of *Golf in the Kingdom* is that Burningbush
is the renowned Old Course at St. Andrews Links, called "golf's greatest stage" whenever a classic tournament is held there. The Old Course
goes back hundreds of years, to the time when the game was played on
windswept seaside land that no one believed was of much use other than
for grazing sheep. The course is so steeped in history and legend that
visitors from around the world travel there as a kind of golf pilgrimage.
I have heard grown men say that they found themselves on the verge of
tears when they took the turn at hole twelve and gazed upon the town
spires of St. Andrews appearing in the distance When my younger
daughter spent a college semester at the University of Edinburgh, I made

At St. Andrews, the penultimate stop in my quest

the trek from California to visit her and took a side trip to that iconic course so that I too could play a game there. I've kept the scorecard and the ball I played with that day in a basket on my study bookshelf, like relics from an epic quest.

As my adulthood golfing passion gained momentum, I took out a faculty membership in Stanford's golf course, avidly read golf writings, watched golf movies, and traveled when I could to play on other ancient courses, including the Massachusetts courses made famous by Updike's *Golf Dreams* (Myopia Hunt Club in South Hamilton) and Bill Paxton's *Greatest Game Ever Played* (The Country Club in Brookline). I introduced myself to Michael Murphy and visited him in his Northern California hometown, where he enlightened me not only about his special perspective on the mysteries of golf but also about his deep insights into psychology and the boundaries of human mental and physical performance. (Another of Murphy's notable achievements is cofounding Esalen Institute in Big Sur, the original embodiment of New Age spiritual values.) My meetings with him expanded my understanding of lifelong human development, and his vision of golf is present throughout this chapter.

Given everything I know about the game—both mystical and practical—and everything I've learned about my father's character, it does not surprise me that my father was a great golfer. One of the secrets of golf is that you must not try too hard—you need to play in that zone between too much and too little attention. In *Golf in the Kingdom*, the golf guru Shivas Irons tells Murphy when he makes a bad shot, "You are trying too hard, Michael." Consistent with Murphy's philosophy and other fascinating writings, *Golf in the Kingdom* explains how a Zen-like detachment works best. You care, but you let it go. Swing easy (the ball actually goes farther that way). Play it as it lays. "Let the course play you," he writes. When things go wrong, just "wait it out" (or "wait it oot," as the Scottish guru says). How perfect this sport was for my father! He was an expert at not trying too hard. Yet when he found something he cared about (his wartime trial witness duty, his foreign service, his second family), he was there for it, and he rose to the occasion. My father mastered golf, an achievement that's eluded legions of strivers who have dedicated years of toil, money, and passion to this elusive effort.

An expert at not trying too hard—how different from my mother was my absent father! Once she realized my father was never coming back and recovered from that blow, my mother ceaselessly worked to better her lot in life (and mine). She paid attention to every detail. She was a bundle of energy. Frequently it was the aggravated kind of energy, which of course was one of the reasons she was hard to get along with. My life review revealed that my father was described as easygoing, underperforming, irresponsible, and "having no filter," both in his schoolboy days and later in adulthood. To use a phrase that did not exist in his time, he was laid-back. Whatever term means the opposite of that word (and I'm not sure there is one) would describe my mother.

Where do I fit in between these two married-but-permanently-separate individuals? It is always tempting to find a middle ground between opposite cases, but I cannot honestly say that this applies to me. With regard to the way I've approached my activities and chances in life—the consequential ones and even the recreational ones—I am far more like my mother than my father, with all the ups and downs that this personality pattern entails. As I've written throughout this book, my life review was an idiographic study that does not lend itself to any generalizations beyond my one case. But in terms of this one case, it stands as an example of the importance of child rearing relative to heredity. My mother raised me, and she acted as a firsthand, live-in role model for me. My father contributed his DNA. This was not nothing: I truly appreciate his doing so, because without this contribution I would not be here! But it did not shape my personality.

Nor, unfortunately, did it impart to me his great golf ability. More on that now.

A Personal Pilgrimage

My initial resentments notwithstanding, I found that imagining my father as a great golfer added more zest to my affection for the sport, and, I must say, the reverse was true as well: my love of golf has made me feel a closer connection to him and a bit like him. Never was this more the case than when I undertook a personal "golf pilgrimage" of sorts, driven by my discoveries.

The first step in my golf pilgrimage happened without initiative on my part. My "new" cousin Chris (one of Aunt Verna's sons) phoned me one day to tell me that hanging long untouched in a Rhode Island family garage was a worn set of golf clubs that had belonged to my father when he was young. Chris heard me gasp. I wanted to see those clubs. At the same time, I found myself wondering, in admiration, *What kind of family has a garage where they keep golf clubs used by family members over seventy years ago?* I stood in awe of that kind of domiciliary continuity. Families that I'd known—including the one that raised me and even the one I've had a hand in raising—felt to me like rootless nomads in comparison.

My good-hearted cousin Chris shipped me the clubs that very week. When the box came, I opened its cardboard packing like an archaeologist excavating a treasure-packed tomb. The clubs lifted easily out of their shipping box. They were in a lightweight canvas golf bag that bore little resemblance to the stout polyester bag I was accustomed to carrying around. The canvas was a weather-beaten tan, with some sparse leather trimming adorning the bottom edge—reminiscent of a safari jacket worn in a Victorian-era desert clime.

The slim bag contained just one pocket, which I eagerly dug into. There I found further treasures: two golf balls and a filled-out scorecard from the Pittsfield Country Club. The golf balls were stamped "Acushnet." As golf lovers know, Acushnet, Massachusetts, is the home of Titleist, the supreme maker of golf balls. The golf division of the Acushnet Process Company began using the brand "Titleist" in 1935, after a pair of MIT-educated rubber specialists designed a golf ball with better balance than those the company had been making. My father was born in 1923. Assuming that the balls in the bag had been acquired around the time the bag was last used (and the balls did appear fairly new), that would put my father's age at around twelve when he was playing with those clubs.

The scorecard told more of the story. On the day that it was marked, my father played with three friends, Emy, Anne, and Scott. On the front nine, my father shot a modest 58, about the same as his friends. Then he went on to play the back nine alone, recording scores for himself but none for his friends. For the back nine, my father shot a strong 43—scorching, actually, for a twelve-year-old playing with stiff, old-fashioned irons, woods with actual wooden heads, and premodern golf balls not yet designed with the good balance that the Titleist Company was soon to produce. My father's scores for those back-nine holes contained four pars, showing his splendid potential.

How did those scores translate into the actual shots my father needed to take as he moved his ball along the fairways of the Pittsfield Country Club? How might I play those holes myself? I was overcome by an urge to see the course where my father learned his game, the land that he trod when he was a boy. I wanted to compare my own ragged grown-up game with his youthful talent. I wanted to play the PCC, as folks in Pittsfield call the lovely hillside course that sits at the feet of the Berkshire Mountains.

It's not easy for outsiders to gain access to private country cubs, but it was my good luck to have a chance connection. Brian Bronk, the husband of a former doctoral student and current friend of mine, Kendall Bronk, had grown up in Pittsfield. As present-day Californians, Brian and I share memories of Massachusetts and an abiding affection for the Red Sox. When he was a child in Pittsfield, Brian had taken golf lessons at the country club and still had friends who were members. He offered me a great favor: to set me up with an introduction to one of his old friends, Matthew Keator, a charming and distinguished young businessman now prominent in the Pittsfield community. Matthew immediately invited me to journey to Pittsfield for a round of golf with him. With my father's scorecard from the 1930s embedded in my mind, it was to be a round of golf with my father.

The Pittsfield Country Club is set on a busy city street less than a mile from the house where my father and Aunt Verna were raised. Before going over to the club, I stopped by the family home, still intact on South Mountain Road. The Damon family lived there until the early 1950s. After the passing of my grandfather and Verna's marriage, my grandmother moved to Boston and rented a full-floor apartment with a claque of women cousins known to all as "the aunts." My father lived in Europe and Thailand after the war, so his childhood home in Pittsfield continued to be the US residence listed in all his records.

I walked around the old Damon house and took a few pictures. No one was there, so I could not see the inside. Although I'd learned that my mother brought me to this house a number of times before I was four, nothing I saw triggered any feelings or memories related to those visits. I have a dim mental image of my grandfather ill in bed during what must have been my last visit, but whether that memory is real or constructed, or some mix of both, I cannot tell.

The drive from the old Damon family house to the Pittsfield Country Club took less than ten minutes. It was a spring day with a deep blue sky, crystal clear air, and a slight wind that brought the fragrance of mountain flowers. When I arrived at the course, I was struck by its sweeping country spaces and sparkling views of mountains overlooking a nearby lake. I recalled, bemusedly, that my father was quoted in Otis Pease's World War II book as deriding the "provincial" atmosphere of the Massachusetts town where he grew up. To me, raised in a dense, grimy factory town, the idyllic spot where my father spent his boyhood seemed enchanted in comparison. It was hard not to feel a twinge of envy. My resentment on learning about my father's golf life came back in full force: Why couldn't the guy at least have come by to give me a lesson or two?

Once on the course, though, my negative feelings lifted. I felt a sense of liberation as I took my first swing. The green mountainous terrain seemed to invite a freewheeling, go-for-it effort. I relaxed immediately, not an easy thing to do when golfing, but the key to everything. From that first drive onward, my fairway shots soared high into the bright blue sky, pausing momentarily at their peak, then dropping softly on the well-manicured country-club grass. Every decent shot—and I had more than my usual share—gave me a thrill. Because I was unfamiliar with the greens, I missed a bunch of easy putts, which put a big dent in my score. But none of my blunders diminished the elation I felt as I traversed the glorious eighteen holes of the course. With its sudden vistas of hills and lakes and its combination of wild and carefully tended scenery, it was unlike any I had encountered. But it did not seem strange or foreign to me. Quite the opposite, I felt right at home. The course seemed to welcome me like a native son.

As for my score—well, the bottom line is that my father, at age twelve or less, outplayed me on most holes. My total score was 93 (roughly my average at the time for playing on an away course), with a 46 on the front nine and a 47 on the back nine. I had five pars overall. I could not match my father's splendid 43 for his back nine, nor his six pars for the eighteen. His total score (101) was higher than mine, but this was due to some blow-up holes on the front nine, including scores of 8s and 9s, when he was fooling around with his friends on the holes they played together. Once he got alone and began to focus, everything changed. At that point, his game outshone mine by a clear margin, even as a twelve-year-old playing with antiquated clubs and balls. If I considered this a talent competition, he came out well on top.

Yet it turned out that my interest in comparing my father's performance with mine was not competitive. My second-hand encounter with my father's early golf talent gave me great satisfaction. When I realized how well he had done on a course that I had played on myself and could envisage clearly, I felt proud and redeemed: proud as anyone might be when someone close accomplishes something notable and redeemed from my immaturely resentful thoughts that the man who fathered me was nothing more than an irresponsible loser. Reconciling those uneasy concerns has been a part—not the whole, but a real part—of what motivated my life-review quest to discover all I could about this man who disappeared from my life at its outset. Golf is a small token when put up against the other marks of my father's achievements that I've dug up in my searches. But it's a significant one for me, which says something about the connection I've found with a man who felt the same way about the Great Game.

8

Reframing Regrets, Finding Gratitude, and Renewing Identity

"REGRETS, I'VE HAD a few, but then again, too few to mention," sang Frank Sinatra, in a line I've smiled at and believed sensible. Before embarking on my life review, I'd never cared to look too closely at the whys and what-ifs of my own life journey. But that spirit, plucky as it may seem, did not serve as a sufficient formula for my psychological well-being. Dealing appropriately with the buried regrets I had was high on my agenda as I began to reexamine my past and uncover its secrets.

Regrets pose the greatest risk to self-acceptance. By definition, regrets indicate choices we wish we hadn't made. For this reason, holding on to regrets can be emotionally destabilizing. Not letting go of regrets can lead to resentment, bitterness, overriding doubt—and, if taken to the extreme, the abiding sense of despair that Erik Erikson warned against. As we look back, regrets that we hold on to can get in the way of our need to affirm the value of our experiences and of life itself.

Yet if we deal with regrets in a positive way, they offer us opportunities for self-renewal and personal improvement. We can learn from the mistakes that our regrets reveal. We can seek to understand why we made those mistakes and choose a different course in the future. Our task as we age is to come to terms with our regrets in a growth-oriented manner rather than stewing over them in a state of dejection.

In a life review, it's important to distinguish between two different types of regrets. There are objective regrets that result from a considered assessment of mistaken actions that had actual consequences, and then there are subjective regrets that result from unsupported speculations about "what might have been." The reason it's important to distinguish these two kinds of regrets is that they need to be treated differently if we are to avoid the emotional pitfalls of unresolved remorsefulness.

The first type of regret follows from a recognition of real mistakes we've made. When we confront such mistakes squarely, we take lessons from them. This is in keeping with the foremost benefit of a life review: the opportunity to examine our past experiences with an eye to what we can learn from them. As I have noted throughout this book, a life review not only can help us understand our pasts; it also can guide our futures by the lessons it contains.

The second type of regret results from "alternative universe" thinking. We imagine roads not taken, conjuring up portraits of a life different from the one we've had. Whether intentionally or not, this pattern of thinking reflects dissatisfaction with the way things have turned out, and it tends to keep that dissatisfaction alive. It also creates barriers to maintaining a positive identity through the ups and downs of events over the years. This what-if pattern of thinking fails to ratify the number one rule of self-acceptance: the events that mark our lives make us the people we are today, and no other configuration of events would have done that.

As I examined my own past, I realized that I had been living with both types of regret. This was a revelation to me: I had buried many of those regrets with a glib "I'm OK" attitude. This worked well enough for functioning purposes but left a legacy of disturbing feelings. My previous approach had been to deny those feelings. That approach proved limited; I was past that now.

Regarding my *objective* regrets, I concluded that I had made some real mistakes that I needed to acknowledge and learn from. One mistake I deeply regretted was not forcing myself to have a conversation with my mother about what really happened with my father. It would have been a painful, embarrassing, drawn-out conversation, and certainly she would have resisted it. It would have taken me well beyond my comfort zone. But I doubt it would have harmed our relationship; in fact, most likely this would have strengthened our bond and opened the door to further beneficial exchanges. Not doing this was a grave mistake because I could never undo it. Once my mother passed, all my chances to find out what she knew and talk with her about her feelings and mine came to an end.

So the first lesson from my life review, for me and virtually everyone with loved ones, is to *make sure to have all the important conversations with loved ones before it's too late.* It may be hard to do. It may feel like pulling teeth. It may be awkward, conflictual, and unwanted. The conversations probably will not end, in Hollywood fashion, with smiles and hugs all around. But such conversations can lead to valuable benefits—for yourself (discovering the full background of your own life course), for your relationships (clearing the air, opening the door to better future communication, building mutual understanding), and for your loved ones (signaling to them that you care enough to extend yourself in a difficult way). This is a message with some urgency. Such conversations are diminishing assets. If not conducted in a timely manner, they lose value and eventually will not be there.

Another of my objective regrets was my failure to follow up on the clues about my father that surfaced from time to time. My most egregious failure in this regard was letting Pichitra's second letter go unanswered during my cluttered midlife. My busy life was no excuse. When I recaptured my memory of that neglect through my life review, I immediately realized how awful a mistake I had made. This became all the more evident to me after I started meeting members of my father's family, beginning with Aunt Verna and her sons (my cousins), Aunt Verna's other relatives, and my father's other daughters (Lawan and Sumali). These are great people who would have enhanced my life enormously had I gotten to know them earlier.

In my younger years, I took much the same unresponsive approach to other, more minor clues that I ignored. The unpleasant lady's comment that "the apple doesn't fall far from the tree" is the one I most clearly remember, but I'm sure there must have been others that I let pass without thought. Certainly the presence of my grandmother in my childhood, sporadic though it was, offered me chances to explore the mystery of my father's absence. But I never did.

The result of all this was my greatest regret of all: I forfeited the possibility of meeting my father and getting to know him while he was alive. Not only was this a loss in itself; it also postponed my chance to know my half sisters, cousins, and Aunt Verna until late in my life. This would have been a most welcome benefit for a boy with very little family at home. Now that I've found out how much I treasure my "new" relatives, this protracted postponement stings all the more.

Getting to know my father would have raised mixed feelings of an uncertain nature, but it would have revealed to me the many ways that the course of his life shaped my own destiny, especially with respect to the all-important matter of my schooling. Learning about this was essential for a valid understanding of exactly how I came to be the person I've been and am now—that is, a true account of my developing identity. My long-standing incuriosity about my father's fate postponed this fundamental self-understanding for decades.

Why this mistaken incuriosity, and what can I learn from it? Here I also turn to my life review to extract lessons. As my school transcripts revealed to me, my stubborn independence goes all the way back. Regarding my missing father, my stubbornness took the form of a defiant stance: "I don't need you!" This was excusable in a boy forced to fend for himself in all the arenas where having a father could have helped (and, as a point of principle, everyone's early tendencies should be "excusable"). But when left unattended for too long, a stubborn streak deters essential learning. It can become a form of pridefulness, a destructive vice, and it obstructs intellectual humility, an essential virtue. My continued stubborn streak nurtured my impenetrable incuriosity and blocked every chance to discover my father and his family.

Our ability to learn relies on open-mindedness, curiosity, humility, and the willingness to take the risk of finding out something that may upset our emotional balance, at least temporarily. In my attitude toward my missing father, I failed to take this risk. Discovering this provided me with a late-life character education.

I also discovered, much to my surprise, that I had long been harboring the second type of regret, more subjective in nature. In my occasional brooding ruminations about my father after I found out that he did not die in the war, I imagined him as a no-account rogue who drifted away to an empty life devoid of achievement or purpose. This untrue image contradicted all the clues that came my way during my youth, culminating in my mother's explicit revelation when I was a sophomore in college. How could my father be paying her child support if he were the aimless vagabond that I imagined? Pichitra's second letter, twenty years later, had revealed to me that my father had a stable second family and notable Foreign Service career. Still, I persisted in my unexamined imaginings of him as drifting detritus. This not only violated the truth of the matter; it also made it impossible for me to understand why he did what he did; and that made it hard for me to forgive him for abandoning my mother and me.

The capacity for forgiveness is another essential character virtue, saving us from the pain of endless grudges and paving the way for reconstituted positive relations with those we forgive. It prevents us from reacting in ways that we then may have trouble forgiving in ourselves. When I first learned, from Pichitra's second letter, that my father was ill, I'm sure I couldn't have cared less. I may even have had a fleeting thought that he deserved it (although I can't say that I remember anything else about my reaction to that long-forgotten letter). In any case, my mistaken views of my father and my unforgiving thoughts were errors that have caused me persistent intellectual confusion and emotional discomfort over the years. I've borne an unadmitted grudge against him, which is the worst kind of grudge, because it cannot be contested. It took a serious life review to clear that up.

The lesson here is that allowing ourselves to retain illusory beliefs unsupported by reality is a form of self-deception, with all the attendant hazards of self-deception. Among the hazards is an inability to grasp actual truths that make possible constructive approaches such as forgiveness. It was only after my life-review discoveries tore apart my illusory deprecations of my father that I was able to extend my understanding and forgiveness to his memory. This was too late to have any value for him, but it proved to be a real relief for my own peace of mind.

In one of my more recent conversations with my wonderful half sister Lawan, she began a sentence with the following phrase: "With all the bad luck that our father had . . ." I don't now remember the rest of her sentence: I'm not even sure I caught it at the time, in the emotional tide of that opening remark. But that one phrase burned into my consciousness and has stayed there ever since. It makes me think of my father struggling with his dire illness for twenty years: in the words of Kenneth MacCormac, "He's totally bedridden. I think he's nearly blind. His only source of happiness is the books on records which he gets from the Library of Congress." My heart now breaks with sympathy. I wish I could do something about it; or, more to the point, I wish I had been around when it mattered to offer him words that might have comforted him, words of his son's life, words of forgiveness, and, if I knew then what I know now, even words of gratitude. It took me a long time and an extended period of life review to be able to feel this way. I am very glad that I do.

Finding Gratitude

A primary purpose of a life review is affirming the value of the life we've been given. This is easy to say in the abstract. But the particulars of any life—and some more than others—can resist affirmation. It is very hard to think positively about the real-life tragedies that blight many lives. Serious illness, the loss of loved ones, wars and civic conflict, economic collapse, and other too-common life disasters can impair the quality of life to the point of enduring misery. Glib sayings such as "everything works out for the best" or "stay on the sunny side of the street" don't suffice to ease the pain of such tragedies. We must find the courage to cope with them and find meaningful ways to survive the damage they have wrought.

Even apart from tragedies, every life has its share of disappointments, wrecked plans, and missed opportunities. Some of these are caused by our own shortcomings. How can we arrive at a sense of serene self-acceptance in the face of such common, often self-inflicted, depredations?

In a life review, the path to self-acceptance leads through gratitude. The logic is this: We've each been given a life on this planet. Some of what's happened during that life was within our control, and some beyond it. We obviously shouldn't hold ourselves to account for outcomes that we cannot control. What a life review can do in this regard is identify the forces beyond our control that have affected us in adverse ways and place them in their proper relation to fortuitous influences that also have marked our lives. This may offer us a path to gratitude if the fortuitous influences have been significant and the tragic outcomes bearable. If, though, the outcomes have been exceedingly tragic, we must mourn them and seek ways to cope with the misery they bring. This is a soul-searching matter that goes beyond the capacity of life review and its self-acceptance agenda.

As for the choices we ourselves have made to exert control over our destinies, naturally we ask ourselves whether they worked out as we hoped.

If we identify mistakes we made that we now regret, we can learn from those in the manner that I noted above. But this will not change the situations we are now living with—that is, the current road that our choices have put us on. How do we think about roads we might have gone down had we made other choices? In a life review, "roads not taken" are seen not as lost opportunities but as passageways that would have deterred us from the lives we eventually forged through the choices we did make. Our actual choices, whatever they were, made us into the persons we are today.

As a rule, people wish to keep their own identities. At times we may envy someone else's situation, but we do not wish to *become* that other person in mind and spirit. As long as we are alive, we remain committed to experiencing life as ourselves, whoever we have become. Realizing this means valuing the choices that produced who we are at present. This is not to say that we should stop seeking improvement. But it is to say that we do appreciate the present selves that we've arrived at. We have compassion for the younger selves that made the choices that led us here today. We own those choices and their outcomes, because there is no person other than ourselves that we could be. This is why we value the choices we've made: they are an integral part of who we now are. Appreciating this essential truth is the key to being grateful for the life we've been given and the choices we've made to shape that life.

Gratitude is much studied these days in psychology because studies have confirmed its many benefits. Research by Robert Emmons and his colleagues has shown that grateful people have stronger bonds with their local communities, more satisfying relationships with friends and relatives, and are better liked. They also have fewer stress-related illnesses, are more physically fit, and have lower blood pressure than non-grateful people. Emmons's experiments have shown that fostering gratitude in subjects improves their subjective and physical well-being. A grateful attitude generates joy, serenity, wonder, and forgiveness. It stimulates learning and sets the stage for thriving. Grateful people tend to receive positive responses from others because they project an air of approval of those around them. Gratitude also can provide resilience during hard times.

This is why gratitude is considered a character strength—it is more than simply a matter of saying "thank you" out of politeness. Gratitude is a cultivated determination to find a positive essence in our life situations. It means becoming aware of the benefits we receive, experiencing appreciation for those benefits, feeling a sense of goodwill toward the source of those benefits, and having a desire to act positively that flows from this appreciation and goodwill. Gratitude can be directed toward other people (friends, coworkers, relatives), transcendent powers (God, nature), or institutions (country, society, school, college). Gratitude has been explicitly identified as a prime virtue in most, if not all, religious traditions. In writings on "civic virtue" it has been recognized as a primary motivator of benevolent behavior.

During my life review, I realized that I had long been harboring doubts: Would I have had a better lot in life with a father to guide me, protect me, set a good example for me, and all the other things a father can do for a son? I firmly buried those doubts when I was young, out of a sense that I would do best by going in the face of them and declaring I could take care of myself just fine. But the doubts were always there, resurfacing whenever I ran into serious problems I had trouble coping with. The doubts would aggravate the problems, adding an unsettling edge of sourness. How could I dispel these long-standing doubts that continued to cloud my sense of positive identity and well-being?

My solution was finding a way to be grateful for the hand my family situation had dealt me. This is what I mean by my claim that the path to self-acceptance leads through gratitude. I did not need to go so far as to convince myself that my past and present conditions have satisfied every possible wish I might have. Nor did I need to believe that "everything worked out for the best" for me in an objective sense. What I did need was to appreciate the ways that my past and present conditions have contributed to all the things I value in my experience and, beyond this, how my past and present situations have set me up to make fulfilling choices for my future.

Developing this appreciation requires understanding how adverse conditions can have compensatory benefits, at least in the psychological sense (just as, in opposite cases, seemingly propitious windfalls, such as winning a fortune in a state lottery, sometimes can bring the winners unhappiness over time). We often find ways to adapt, and even thrive, when we find ourselves in unfortunate circumstances. Occasionally such adaptations make us stronger in an objective sense: legions of star athletes overcame physical handicaps in their youth, the ranks of top business leaders are replete with people who struggled with dyslexia and other learning disorders, and so on. In other cases, our adaptations are subjective—we learn to live contentedly with conditions that we can't change. The clinical literature on people who have accidents that suddenly turn them into paraplegics has reported that after about a year of adjustment, such people often attain states of subjective well-being (the psychological term for happiness) similar to what they had before their accidents. Psychological states, as philosophers as far back as the Stoics realized, are not inexorably linked to our objective conditions.

As Henry David Thoreau wrote, "If we will be quiet and ready enough, we shall find compensation in every disappointment." My life review revealed multiple ways, large and small, that my father's absence was compensated for in my objective or subjective experience. Objectively, I learned to fend for myself in ways that I may not have done had my father been there to look out for me. In comparing my schooling with his (at the same school and college), I found that my father's experience of secure (very likely overindulgent) parenting, pleasant as it must have been, likely turned him into an indolent underperformer. In contrast, the hardscrabble environment I was raised in nurtured an ambition that served me well in the competitive circles of my education and early career. As for my family life, after reviewing my mother's nature and my own in relation to the picture I've been able to sketch of my father's nature, I now believe that his return home would not have ended well for any of us. It's impossible for me to imagine how he could have gotten along with my mother for even a short period of time, let alone sustain their marriage. As for him and me, I see inevitable conflict. I was told once that he fought often with his daughter Pichitra because of her independent streak. From what I can discern, Pichitra was a sweetheart, especially in comparison to me when I was young. How would my father have dealt with an exceedingly difficult wife and a relentlessly stubborn son? I am now glad that I was not put in a position to find out.

Not to put an overly rosy gloss on my situation, there indeed were objective losses that I suffered due to my father's absence. There were huge gaps in my knowledge of how to become an adult male that I needed to make up for throughout my youth. Some were minor—learning how to tie a necktie, how to shave, how to ride a bike and drive a car—that I figured out on my own after some embarrassing bumbling. Others were more difficult and more important. When I had children of my own, I needed to learn for myself how to be a father, without having a role model from my own youth. I'm sure I also missed some career opportunities along the way without a father to share with me his knowledge of how the world works.

Yet regarding such objective losses, I have found compensatory psychological benefits on the subjective front. As an example, I'll cite golf one last time. I could use swimming, or ice skating, or gardening, or reading, or any other avocation for this example, but I've started with golf for this book so I'll stick with it. My experience playing the game has been touched by revelations of what my missing father was like. To the point I am making here, my subjective compensations for the missing gaps in my golf game are emblematic of my quest to find gratitude in the course of my life review as a whole.

Since childhood, golf has been a source of joy and fascination. The quality of my game matters. I've tried to improve it over the years, mostly on my own (out of stubbornness or thrift, I've never taken a paid lesson, though I do listen to tips from playing partners). My efforts have met with no more than modest results: I can make all sorts of good shots but lack the skilled consistency required for really good scores. There's no doubt in my mind that I'd be a far better golfer if my father had been there to tutor me when I was starting out. I wouldn't have needed to unlearn the bad habits I acquired in my untutored ignorance and would have picked up good practices I could have honed over the years, leading to true golfing proficiency. Imagining this thrills me. That it will never happen is a real, objective loss.

But as I consider this objective loss, I also think about the multitude of better golfers I've played with who evince despair whenever their games fall short of perfection (which every golfer's game does with annoying regularity). Frustration, agony, and horror are firmly embedded in the emotional baggage of many superb golfers whenever their shots go awry. Often, despite their excellence, they don't really feel great about the game they are playing.

Not so with me. With all my mediocrity, I thoroughly enjoy every moment of my time on a golf course. I marvel at my good shots and laugh off my terrible ones. When a bad shot puts me in trouble in the rough, I get a kick out of seeing if I can save the day with a miracle rescue play. My reliable enjoyment of the game is a result of my low expectations for myself—which in turn result from the middling game I've been left with in the absence of instruction. My enchantment with golf has taken me on far-flung adventures that have enhanced my life enormously.

Whether or not I would have become similarly enchanted under my father's tutelage is impossible to say. On the one hand, from my present perspective, I thrill at the idea of learning the game well and also at the thought that I could have shared a common fascination with the father I never had. On the other hand, in my studies I've observed many young people who lose interest in the activities their parents introduce them to because these young people wish to acquire interests they can call their own. I can't say which way I would have responded. But whatever the case, I can say that I would not want to change anything about the way I now relate to the game. I am delighted that it is what it is. I am grateful that things have turned out this way for me.

Generalizing this message beyond the "Great Game," I learned in the conduct of my life review to see other parts of my past and present in a similar way. Whenever there was objective loss, there also were compensations—some objective, others subjective—that I've been able to recognize. My awareness of such compensations supports the essential belief that I have much to be grateful for. This belief is profoundly important. A life review's goal of renewing identity to prepare for a positive future enhanced by such gratitude.

Renewing Identity

In our spontaneous everyday thinking, we frequently take stock of our lives. We do this when we wonder whether we are in the right jobs, or in the right relationships, or dwelling in the place that best suits us. We take stock of our lives when we size up our financial assets, or when we assess our contributions to our families, our professional fields, or the world at large. We take stock of our lives when we ask ourselves whether we are happy or discontented or when we wonder whether we've been foolish or wise. For most people, this happens regularly. Usually it entails no more than a brief reflection on personal conditions or characteristics that have become salient at the moment.

There are times, however, when taking stock has special meaning and calls for a mindful, sustained effort. Major transitions—such as graduation from school, a marriage or a divorce, the loss of a loved one, a health crisis leading to physical incapacity, a new job or a retirement—all can trigger such efforts. These and other junctures in life's journey require us to mentally adapt to new circumstances. Some junctures may be full of promise (graduation, marriage, a new job), while others may be tinged with foreboding (a health crisis, a financial reversal, even retirement for many people). Whether or not the new circumstances are welcome, preparing for them means taking stock of who we are and who we can become under the changed conditions. This involves renewing identity, reaffirming the parts that have served us well, and revising or adding to them as needed. It is a process of sizing up and recalibrating an identity for a future that will bring new challenges and opportunities. Although the future will be different from the past and present, there will be continuities as well. Our identities remain continuous in some ways but must change in other ways as we reexamine them in light of new circumstances.

Adapting our identities to match these changed circumstances is key to personal growth and thriving. For a young person entering adulthood, this means incorporating roles such as worker, parent, and citizen into his or her identity. For an older person leaving the workplace, this means finding new purposes, age-appropriate lifestyle arrangements, and other ways of aging gracefully. For people at any age, adapting to changing circumstances requires a mental check-in, leading to some confirmation, as well as some adaptation and transformation, of their present identities in order to meet their futures.

Identity growth does not happen randomly, like arbitrary scribbles on an empty canvas. Like every sort of psychological development, identity growth builds on established concepts, and to a large extent whatever is added takes its direction from these earlier concepts. As the developmental theorist Heinz Werner once remarked, "Something is not coming out of nothing." This is why understanding the past is so important for well-directed identity growth. Knowing where we have been gives us conscious control over where we are going and who we will be. When, through my life review, I recaptured the roots of my career choices (research and writing focused on human development and moral commitment), it gave me fresh determination to extend that thread into my future activities and new ideas about how I could share this purpose with others. I also took a hard look at my efforts that hadn't worked—inauthentic endeavors, wrong turns, false leads—and thought about how I could do better. Knowing what has given us purpose in our pasts strengthens our agency in adapting ourselves to the inevitable transitions we face. The better we understand our pasts, the wiser our choices about our future directions.

A life review is a special effort to take conscious control over our personal identities and their future directions. It adds reflection and information to a process that happens spontaneously as we age. Identities change over time, and, as I've noted, such change is always informed by our past experience. But for most of us, important segments of the past are obscured by limitations in our memories, lack of key facts, or (as in my case) closely held family secrets. One of the values of a life review is in retrieving the important parts of our pasts for our present awareness. Ideally, the clarity and understanding achieved through this retrieval will add to our capacities to guide the shape and substance of our future selves. Another potential benefit of a life review—when it is enhanced by a search for gratitude—is that it can help us affirm the worth of the life we've led, while accepting frankly all that did not work out as hoped and planned.

These two potential benefits of a life review—a well-directed path to a hopeful future and a positive take on one's past and present—can be crucial for anyone attaining maturity. Robert Butler, inventor of the life-review approach, had older people in mind, especially those battling depression. Erik Erikson, whose writings on identity development through the life span inspired Butler's approach, also had older people in mind when he asserted the importance of affirming the worth of our lives in order to gain "ego integrity" and prevent lasting despair. Butler also made a point of noting that a life review could be worthwhile for nonclinical populations; and the notion of identity renewal at all ages is consistent with both Butler's and Erikson's theories. Although the only evidence I have to support their claims is my own single case, I can say that my experience with a life review, conducted for a nonclinical purpose and prior to old age, brought me both benefits.

If anything, I wish I had started a life review earlier. I lived too long with unresolved (and largely denied) feelings about growing up fatherless, with mistaken notions about how I took the schooling path that led me to my vocational purpose, and without contact with members of my family who would have been a great joy to know. The information that my life review uncovered resolved those feelings, revealed the truth about my father, corrected my false assumptions about my own developmental trajectory, and enhanced my present-day family relationships. As much as I welcome those benefits, I regret that I waited so long to grasp them.

Yet, like all regrets, even this one turns out to have compensatory factors. Once when I was in the initial flush of excitement about my new discoveries, a friend commented to me, "Bill, thank God that you've discovered all this about your dad, and thank God that you didn't find out about this earlier than you did." I was puzzled by his comment at the time and still am not sure I completely agree with it. But I do know what my friend meant, and he had a point—two points, actually. First, if I had started on my discovery quest while my mother was alive, it would have hurt her deeply. To this day, I'm not sure what I would—or should, or could—have done about that, but it would have been terribly trying for both of us. Second, if I discovered my father when I was young and managed to have a relationship with him, I would not be the person I am now. My relationship with my faraway father likely would have been vexed. If I had been very young, I may have developed a counterproductive identification with him. My mother would have been looking on with anger, and my rebellious streak might have kicked in to aggravate the situation. Who knows how these heated dynamics would have affected me during my formative years? What's more, in the life I did have, I managed to pick up life skills and strengths in learning to cope without a father, a compensatory factor that my life review has now made me aware of and grateful for.

A Personal Pilot Study

For me, it took a dramatic revelation—my daughter's consequential call—to trigger an interest in reviewing my life. I was fortunate to have read writings on the life review approach by Robert Butler and his followers and the groundbreaking scientific research by Dan McAdams and his colleagues on life stories, narrative identity, and personality development. I did not wish to adopt a formal scientific method for the examination of my own life, because I was more interested in the particular patterns in my one unique life than in general patterns that cut across individuals. Accordingly, I made up less formal investigatory procedures as I went along. Much of what I did was mostly common sense: examining old memories and taking notes on whatever I could recall; retrieving my and my father's old school records; contacting friends and relatives who knew me and my family when I was young; meeting with my father's still-living friends and relatives and asking them what they knew; searching historical archives for records of my father's military and foreign service; and using the internet to locate my "new" family members and fill in gaps left by the absence of paper records and the deaths of key players in the story. When possible, I tried to validate the information I uncovered by cross-checking the accounts across my disparate sources. This was an uneven process, bearing no claims to reliability in a scientific sense. The inevitable vagaries of memory leave remaining uncertainties to the life story I was able to come up with.

For this and other reasons, I do not consider my approach a method that is ready for adoption in psychological research or practice. Rather, it is a demonstration case, a pilot study of sorts, with only one subject: me. I found the experience to be valuable personally and intriguing for my professional thinking as a developmental psychologist. I would be pleased to see others in my field explore the potential of the life review approach in rigorous studies with representative samples of subjects. I believe that the pioneering work by Butler and his followers on all varieties of life review, "guided autobiography," "structured recollection," and what's been called "the art and science of reminiscing" offer promising insights about human flourishing that warrant systematic exploration. While I have not tried to do this in my informal use of the life review, I do hope that my experience may be informative to those interested in systematically exploring these promising routes to flourishing in the middle and later periods of life.

A life review is by nature purposeful, because it is an intentional effort to retrieve events that confirm the meaning of a person's life and the purposes which that person has found and pursued over the years. In my use of the life review approach, I had multiple purposes in mind—three personal and one professional.

My first personal purpose was discovering my father and his life story, a purpose that was triggered by the call from my daughter Maria. That call uncovered deeply buried family secrets and swept me up in a fascination that fueled a multiyear discovery quest. I was intrigued by the life of the man who fathered me and then disappeared from my life forever. As I began finding out more about him, my interest extended to his second family, his military service and diplomatic work, and the historical period that he lived through. The story of my father's life is intertwined with the history of his times. This can be said of everyone, of course, but my father's historical entwinement was particularly dramatic and colorful. It spurred my fascination further, and it is one of the reasons my father's story plays such a big part in this book.

My second personal purpose was getting to know my father's family, after I figured out who they were and how much I had missed by neglecting them all those years. I can say without exaggeration that every one of them was wonderfully receptive to developing relationships with me, my wife, and my children and that I found all of them to be great people, interesting, fun to be with, kind and considerate, and full of special talents and unique experiences. Once I got over how much I'd missed by waiting so long to meet them, I've allowed myself to thoroughly enjoy this outcome of my life review.

The third personal purpose of my life review was getting to know myself. This purpose is common among people as we age and realize that we may not have understood the events in our pasts that have made us into the individuals we have come to be. People change over time in ways they may not fully appreciate. For me, understanding my life story and the changes that brought me to my present state meant discovering how my father's life story affected my own. When Maria's call triggered my quest, I was at a time in life when I was ready to do this anyway, similar to everyone looking for the kind of self-renewal and life affirmation that Butler and Erikson wrote about. Maria's call came at a fine moment for me. I could have benefited from doing it earlier, but better late than never. Learning the truth at last, along with the benefits that flowed from that, showed me the value of improving self-knowledge at each and every phase of life.

My fourth, professional, purpose was to try out for myself an approach to identity reconstruction and self-renewal that emerged in my field (life-span developmental psychology) about twenty years ago but has not yet been given the attention I believe it deserves. The approach relies on the telling of life stories. Beginning in the 1990s, significant research and writings have explored this and closely related approaches, but this body of work has not yet made a significant mark on the mainstream of psychological and developmental science. In contrast, in the humanities and related disciplines there has been great interest in personal storytelling in recent years. The popularity of this activity is reflected in StoryCorps, an organization whose mission is to "record, preserve, and share the stories of Americans from all backgrounds and beliefs." The success of StoryCorps and similar initiatives confirms the appeal of telling life stories, and the work of Butler and his followers shows the potential of storytelling as a psychological method for identity reflection and growth. I was intrigued by the possibilities I saw in this new psychological approach and wanted to try it out for myself.

As a helping profession, psychology from its inception has sought ways to counsel people for navigating the challenges of self-discovery and eventual "ego integrity." The original stabs at a solution to such challenges consisted of attempts to relieve psychological suffering by focusing almost solely on unresolved conflicts of the *past*. Sigmund Freud famously dredged the depths of patients' memories in order to repair old injuries that had never healed because they had been suppressed rather than recognized for what they were. The idea behind this "reconstruction work" was that cleaning up a painful history could help disinfect wounds that were still hurting, now perhaps even more intensely than at the time they were inflicted.

Psychology's "cognitive revolution" in the latter half of the twentieth century directed more attention to a person's *present* mode of experiencing the world. Cognitive psychologists were uncomfortable with the idea that people are chained to their pasts and driven by events that they can't even remember. The cognitive view of human nature is more active and more skill-based. If people can be encouraged to think about their lives in more rational, stable, and positive ways, they become better able to cope with problems and seize opportunities in the present. What else, the approach implies, do we actually need for healthy psychological functioning? This cognitive approach, embodied most notably in cognitive behavioral therapy (CBT), has been reinforced by compatible spiritual ideas and practices from Eastern traditions. Meditation and various forms of yoga emphasize the value of *"being present,"* and they offer engaging methods of focusing the mind toward that end. For those who appreciate classical philosophy in the Western tradition, CBT shares the Stoic belief in the power to define, control, and improve experiences by building strong habits of mind and employing these habits to gain emotional stability in the present.

Most recently, psychology's focus has shifted to the influence of the future—or at least future aspirations—on identity and self-development. The theoretical foundations for this focus have been established by psychologist Martin Seligman's writings on what he calls "prospective thinking." The overarching idea is that by imagining hopeful future prospects we can shape our development in more agentic and adaptive ways than we can by dwelling on past problems, and to a much more salutary effect. In this view, counterintuitively, the future is a more important influence on human development than the past or present. Humans are "drawn into the future" by the power of their imaginations, and in the end this is truly what shapes our destinies. This idea is compatible with Seligman's "positive psychology" movement, which emphasizes higher human capacities such as creativity and spirituality.

My own writings on the development of purpose are most closely aligned with the notion of prospective thinking and Seligman's positive psychology approach. Purpose is future-oriented by nature. Purposeful people look ahead to goals they seek to accomplish over the long haul. The power of purpose lies in the strengths that this forward-looking commitment brings: motivation, energy, hope, and resilience. Purpose is a prime example of how a person's future aspirations can shape the person's self-development. This is a liberating point: our destinies are not forever determined by events from our pasts, however forceful or even traumatic. Our thoughts and our imaginations give us personal agency over the direction our lives and our identities will take.

Still, our pasts do matter, and it is essential to attend to present experience as well. Each school of psychology has an essential point to make: past, present, and future all play a part in shaping a person's perspectives on self. The distinctions between the past-, present-, and future-oriented approaches to psychology tell us more about the history of the field than they do about the actual process of self-development. The message we should take from psychology's disparate approaches is that *all* the times of our lives, from our forgotten origins to our imagined futures, provide us with material for self-definition and potential growth. It is up to us to actively search through this material and integrate what we find into a coherent, authentic, and gratifying vision of who we have been, who we are, and who we aim to be as we age and grow.

The possibilities of personal growth remain open-ended for our entire lives if we continue reflecting on the purposes we wish to pursue and the identities we wish to build. But real growth takes time, and it rarely proceeds in a straight line. Psychological development takes many twists and turns and encompasses paradoxes that defy simple formulations. In my professional work as a developmental psychologist, I have been especially intrigued by this complex, long-term, and often paradoxical nature of developmental change. Exploring this has been one of the pleasures of working in my field, and my present exploration has proven to be no exception.

Finally, my life review revealed four paradoxes in the quest to develop a fulfilling self-identity with integrity and purpose:

1. The capacity for looking forward in a positive way requires looking backward in an open and frank way, acknowledging and coming to terms with regrets and negative occurrences.

2. Autobiographical discovery deepens a person's understanding of self; but at the same time it relies on the person's knowledge of others who have influenced the formation of self, often in previously unknown ways.

3. Identity with integrity requires taking seriously what we have done, what we are doing, and what we will choose to do ("everything matters"); but taking ourselves too seriously can lead to exaggerated self-importance and detrimental self-absorption: humility is essential in reviewing the course of any individual life.

4. Purpose is beneficial for the self because it demands a commitment to accomplish aims that are beneficial for the world *beyond* the self: this is how purpose fosters resilience and energy while detering lethargy and self-absorption.

Every choice we make in life flows in some way from our sense of who we are and who we want to be. This is why self-identity is such a powerful force in our everyday lives. It shapes every risk we take, every aspiration we aim to achieve, and every mundane or noble purpose we pursue. Self-identity is not given to us at birth. We can intentionally work on revising our self-identities, out of a sense that we can (and should) determine the kinds of people we become. When we do this, we play an active role in inventing our own futures.

ACKNOWLEDGMENTS

The advice, support, and information provided to me by family, friends, colleagues, and helpful people I met along the way made this book possible. My first thanks go to my daughter Maria Damon for taking the initiative of uncovering the mysteries of my father's life story for me to explore. I thank Maria and her sister, Caroline Damon, for visits and interviews in Thailand with my father's wife and family there. As for my father's birth and second family—the American and Thai branches both—I am enormously grateful for their generosity and their welcoming reception of me when I introduced myself to them. My primary debt is to my father's younger sister, Verna Matthews, who, sadly, has recently departed. Verna not only became an important source for this book but also a wonderful aunt to me in the seven short years that I had to know her. I miss Verna and think of her often. Verna's sons, Chris and Kai, have become my terrific "new" cousins, and they have been great sources of insight and emotional support. Similarly, my "new" half sisters, Sumali and Lawan, provided me with accounts of our father that have been essential to my quest. Just as important, they've become treasured additions to my family life. I have greatly valued my time with them and their fabulous children, Albert, Philip, Prae, and Phoom.

My research for this book included interviews, online searches, and visits to libraries and archives in this country and abroad. My search for school records succeeded due to the efforts of Paige Roberts, the director of Archives and Special Collections at Phillips Academy. Paige is my idea of an archivist from heaven. I also received valued institutional assistance from Harvard, the Archdiocese of Boston, the British War Museum, and the National Personnel Records Service.

I am not a historian by training, and I had much to learn about historical research. I thank Eric Wakin, director of the Hoover Institution library and archives, for his invaluable help in my research on Thai-American relations during my father's time in the Foreign Service there. James Harney, librarian at the Harvard Club of New York City, found for me Julian Bach's *America's Germany*, which gave me the vivid sense I needed of the US postwar occupation of Germany and my father's role in it. The Harvard Club of NYC also keeps alumni reports that I drew on to trace the whereabouts of my father and his college roommates over the years.

I also had a lot to learn about narrative interview techniques and nonfiction storytelling. As for my interview techniques, I thank Elsa Walsh for suggestions that enabled me to salvage key facts that otherwise would have remained undiscovered. Ellen Daly was the best imaginable coach for narrative writing: I enjoyed working with her tremendously and benefited constantly from her sensible advice. For my pilgrimage to Pittsfield, Massachusetts, to play on my father's childhood golf course, I thank my friends Kendall and Brian Bronk, and Matthew Keator, for their gracious help.

Iza Warner has been the finest possible source of information I could have had regarding my father's Germany years. Iza's sparkling accounts were a total joy to hear, in addition to being right on point to what I was seeking. Getting to know Iza and her wonderful daughters Barbara and Daphne was one of the true pleasures of my family search. My Uncle Richard and Aunt Phyllis, and my mother's cousin, Gerry, also provided me with important information. Richard and Gerry have passed away since my meetings with them, as have most in my father's cohort. A lively discussion with my father's second wife, Genevieve Lespagnol Damon, provided me with a vivid, first-hand sense of how the couple met in Germany and their subsequent life together in Thailand. It was truly a moving experience to hear Genevieve—the epitome of a grande dame—speak warmly of her years with my father. Sadly, she, too, passed on just as this book was going to press.

In the discussion of my career development in chapter 6, I include sections from "My Research Life and Times," a chapter that I wrote for *The Developmental Science of Adolescence: History through Autobiography*, edited by R. M. Lerner, A. C. Petersen, R. K. Silbereisen, and J. Brooks-Gunn and published by Psychology Press. I thank Helen Pritt, publisher for Routledge Psychology, for her gracious communications with me to secure permission to use this material for the present book. An early account of my golf experiences appeared in the British magazine *Psychology in Practice* in its December 13, 2019, issue, and I thank Nikki Lucas-Krol, head of publishing, for arranging that preliminary publication.

I was fortunate to have spectacular help in the writing phase of this book. Susan Arellano, my cherished editor for three previous books, once again offered her splendid editorial vision at every step in the writing process. The supreme literary agent Jim Levine helped me formulate the direction of this book project from its inception. Jim also introduced me to Ellen Daly, who, as I noted, gave me welcome advice about narrative storytelling and provided astute first-round edits. Dan Reilly offered excellent suggestions about title and chapter ordering. I thank friends John Osborn, Bob King, Michael Grossmann, Tom Rosenstiel, John Gomperts, Connie Wolfe, and Marc Freedman for suggestions and support that made key differences at one point or another. My fabulous office staff of Lisa Staton and Elissa Hirsh provided noteworthy help for my research for this book project. And I thank Anne Colby for just about everything related to this book, and all else.

NOTES

Chapter 1

3 **It was an interview:** The USIA was a "cultural" wing of the State Department. It was dedicated to spreading the best aspects of the American democratic tradition and lifestyle to any country that might be derailed by the appeals of communism or other totalitarian systems. The term "cultural," of course, contains multitudes: the arts, geographical descriptions, news coverage, political commentary, and covert propaganda. The USIA gathered information on the countries where it was stationed, and often it was said to be in contact with other US intelligence agencies.

4 **He was part of the "Greatest Generation":** T. Brokaw, *The Greatest Generation* (New York: Random House, 1998).

Chapter 2

34 **Frankl wrote his landmark:** V. E. Frankl, *Man's Search for Meaning: An Introduction to Logo-Therapy* (Boston: Beacon, 1959).

35 **The field of psychology:** See, for example, M. E. P. Seligman and M. Csikszentmihalyi, "Positive Psychology: An Introduction," *American Psychologist* 55 (2000): 5–14; and M. E. P. Seligman, T. A. Steen, N. Park, and C. Peterson, "Positive Psychology Progress: Empirical Validation of Interventions," *American Psychologist* 60 (2005): 410–421.

38 **The approach entails:** See, for example, B. Haight and J. Webster, eds., *The Art and Science of Reminiscing: Theory, Research, Methods, and Applications* (Washington, DC: Taylor and Francis, 1995); D. Rubin, ed., *Remembering Our Past* (New York: Cambridge University Press, 1996); James E. Birren, ed., *Aging and Biography* (New York: Springer, 2004); J. E. Birren and D. E. Deutchman, *Guiding Autobiography Groups for Older Adults* (Baltimore and London: Johns Hopkins University Press, 1991); D. McAdams, "The

Psychology of Life Stories," *Review of General Psychology* 5, no. 2 (2001): 100–122; E. Bohlmeijer, M. Roemer, P. C. Smit, and F. Smit, "The Effects of Reminiscence on Psychological Well-Being in Older Adults: A Meta-Analysis," *Aging and Mental Health* 11, no. 3 (2007): 291–300; U. M. Staudinger, "Life Reflection: A Social-Cognitive Analysis of Life Review," *Review of General Psychology* 5 (2): 148–160; D. P. McAdams and K. C. McLean, "Narrative Identity," *Current Directions in Psychological Science* 22, no. 3 (2013): 233–238; Stanton Wortham, "Narrative Self-Construction and the Nature of Self," in *Narratives in Action* (New York: Teachers College Press, 2001), 136–156; J. M. Adler, W. L. Dunlop, R. Fivush, J. P. Lilgendahl, J. Lodi-Smith, D. P. McAdams, K. C. McLean, M. Pasupathi, and M. Syed, "Research Methods for Studying Narrative Identity: A Primer," *Social Psychological and Personality Science*, 8 (2017): 519–527.

39 **Among the psychological benefits:** R. Butler, "Foreword: The Life Review," in *The Art and Science of Reminiscing: Theory, Research, Methods, and Applications*, ed. B. Haight and J. Webster (Washington, DC: Taylor and Francis, 1995), xvii.

40 **McAdams's life-story interview method:** For the Life Story Interview method created by Dan McAdams and his colleagues at Northwestern University, see his "Study of Lives Research Group" website on its "Instruments" webpage: https://sites.northwestern.edu/thestudyoflives researchgroup/instruments/.

40 **Although my focus:** This is the distinction between "nomothetic" and "idiographic" studies that the great psychologist Gordon Allport introduced early in the twentieth century. Nomothetic study, of which the research of Dan McAdams is a brilliant example, looks for patterns that explain general trends in an entire population, whereas idiographic study, of which this book is an example, examines single cases in order to find patterns that explain that case. Of course, each type of study can inform the other. My study in this book has been deeply influenced by findings from nomothetic research, and I hope that it will be informative to those investigating broad patterns of human development.

40 **Research using storytelling:** Willoughby Tavernier, "Adolescent Turning Points: The Association between Meaning-Making and Psychological Well-Being," *Developmental Psychology* 48, no. 4 (2012): 1058–1068.

40 **This suggestive research:** J. J. Bauer, D. P. McAdam, and A. R. Sakaeda, "Interpreting the Good Life: Growth Memories in the Lives of Mature, Happy People," *Journal of Personality and Social Psychology* 88, no. 1 (2005): 203–217; M. Pinquart and S. Forstmeier, "Effects of Reminiscence Interventions on Psychosocial Outcomes: A Meta-Analysis," *Aging and Mental Health* (2012): 1–18.

41 **Birren and his colleagues guided people's autobiographies:** James Birren and Betty Birren, "Autobiography: Exploring the Self and Encouraging Development," in *Aging and Biography*, ed. James E. Birren (New York: Springer, 2004), 34–48.

41 **He quotes Hemingway's observation:** Birren and Birren, "Autobiography," 28.

41 **Life reviews can be useful:** Timothy Hoyt and Monisha Pasupathi, "The Development of Narrative Identity in Late Adolescence and Emergent Adult," in *Developmental Psychology* 45, no. 2 (2009): 558–574; Jack Bauer and Dan McAdams, "Personal Growth in Adults' Stories of Life Transitions," *Journal of Personality* 72, no. 3 (2004): 573–602.

43 **"Emotional events in a family":** R. Butler, "Foreword: The Life Review," in *The Art and Science of Reminiscing: Theory, Research, Methods, and Applications*, ed. B. Haight and J. Webster (Washington, DC: Taylor and Francis, 1995), xx–xxi.

49 **"Our past can be":** Paul T. P. Wong, "The Process of Adaptive Reminiscences," in *The Art and Science of Reminiscing: Theory, Research, Methods, and Applications*, ed. B. Haight and J. Webster (Washington, DC: Taylor and Francis, 1995), 23–24.

Chapter 3

51 **"You can't connect the dots looking forward":** For Steve Jobs's Stanford commencement address, see "You've Got to Find What You Love," *Stanford News*, June 14, 2005, https://news.stanford.edu/2005/06/14/jobs-061505/.

52 **Some disastrous events:** For an insightful treatment of handling hard-to-bear life catastrophes, see D. Van Tongeren and S. Vantongeren, *The Courage to Suffer: A New Clinical Framework for Life's Greatest Crises* (West Conshohocken, PA: Templeton Press, 2020).

57 **Recent writings in medicine:** See, for example, Atul Gawande, *Being Mortal: Medicine and What Matters in the End* (New York: Henry Holt & Co., 2014).

59 **It is rare:** W. Damon, *The Path to Purpose: How Young People Find Their Calling in Life* (New York: The Free Press, 2008). For studies across the world that have reported similar findings, see also Stanford Center on Adolescence, https://coa.stanford.edu/.

59 **Studies have revealed:** Damon, *Path to Purpose*. For studies across the world that have reported similar findings, see also Stanford Center on Adolescence, https://coa.stanford.edu.

59 **Peter Benson:** Peter Benson, *Sparks: How Parents Can Help Ignite the Hidden Strengths of Teenagers* (San Francisco: Jossey-Bass, 2008).

64 **Because of this opportunity:** See Marc Freedman's work at Encore.org, https://encore.org/.

64 **Our Stanford research team:** M. J. Bundick, K. Remington, E. Morton, and A. Colby, "The Contours of Purpose beyond the Self in Midlife and Later Life," *Applied Developmental Science*, 1–21, DOI: 10.1080/10888691 .2018.1531718.

66 **The likelihood that a boy from Brockton:** This says more about my Brockton circles than about Phillips Academy. To the school's long-standing credit, it has always welcomed "striving" boys without means. The school's charter, composed in 1778, commits the school to educating "youth from every quarter." The school has held true to that mission. Nevertheless, it is likely that a boy from my circles never would have known about the school without some out-of-the-ordinary family connection.

Chapter 4

70 **Nowhere did this feel:** In the years since my reunion visit, the school has renovated its hallowed library and moved the archives over to the basement of the campus's central building. For the sake of the entrancing aura that surrounded my visit, I am glad that this change did not come sooner.

71 **A perfectly good definition of character:** At Lexico.com: https://www .lexico.com/definition/character.

76 **"Non Sibi":** As I wrote these words, it also occurred to me that my writings on the importance of "beyond-the-self" purposes may hark all the way back to the character training I received in my Andover years.

76 In a recent book about the Bush family: Peter Schweizer and Rochelle Schweizer, *The Bushes: Portrait of a Dynasty* (New York: Doubleday, 2017).

76 "The school was committed": Schweizer and Schweizer, *The Bushes*, 64.

84 He appears to have developed: A. Duckworth, *Grit: The Power of Passion and Perseverance* (New York: Scribner, 2016).

87 As for our gregariousness: Richard M. Lerner, *Concepts and Theories of Human Development* (Oxford: Taylor and Francis, 2018).

91 Eventually, he took on his: W. Damon, *The Path to Purpose: How Young People Find Their Calling in Life* (New York: The Free Press, 2008); Duckworth, *Grit*.

Chapter 5

106 Although there's no existing record: Such a record would have been filed in the National Personnel Records Center (NPRC) in Saint Louis, Missouri. But on July 12, 1973, a fire there destroyed sixteen million files documenting the service history of military personnel discharged from 1912 to 1964. My father's official files were among them.

107 He also developed: A. Duckworth, *Grit: The Power of Passion and Perseverance* (New York: Scribner, 2016).

111 In my writings on moral development: W. Damon and A. Colby, *The Power of Ideals: The Real Story of Moral Choice* (New York: Oxford University Press, 2015); A. Colby and W. Damon, *Some Do Care: Contemporary Lives of Moral Commitment* (New York: The Free Press, 1992).

Chapter 6

118 "After twelve years of the worst dictatorship": J. Bach, *America's Germany: An Account of the Occupation* (New York: Random House, 1946), 11.

118 "Disrupted transportation": Bach, *America's Germany*, 99.

119 "to 'recover' the German hearts and minds": Bach, *America's Germany*, 4.

120 "The kids are in a muddle": Bach, *America's Germany*, 151.

120 The films had been chosen: Bach, *America's Germany*, 229.

127 "I think it will become equally clear": R. Jeffers, *The Double Axe* (New York: Random House, 1947), viii.

128 **When my father was transferred to Thailand:** Daniel Fineman, *A Special Relationship: The United States and Military Government in Thailand, 1947–1958* (Honolulu: University of Hawai'i Press, 1997).

130 **One of the authoritative biographies:** Paul Handley, *The King Never Smiles* (New Haven, CT: Yale University Press, 2006).

130 **"Phil Damon, who worked for USIS":** Medium.com. https://medium.com /@robertrochlen/in-1956-kukrits-wife-or-ex-wife-who-worked-for-usis-with -my-father-told-my-father-that-the-4d2d61b0ad5e.

135 **In this way she combined her legacy:** Brockton, Massachusetts, was once known as "the shoe capital of the world" due to its seventy humming shoe factories. Not long ago I saw a 1920s silent film in which a placard reading "Buy your Brockton shoes here!" adorned a New York City street scene. By the time I was born, most of Brockton's shoe companies had relocated to the South or gone bankrupt, victims of high New England labor costs and the Great Depression. The city they left behind was still wallowing in economic depression during my childhood there.

139 **In my professional field:** See, for example, N. J. Cabrera and C. S. Tamis-LeMonda, eds., *Handbook of Father Involvement: Multidisciplinary Perspectives* (Oxford: Taylor and Francis, 2013); H. S. Goldstein, "Fathers' Absence and Cognitive Development of Children over a 3- to 5-Year Period," *Psychological Reports* 52, no. 3: 971–976; M. Shinn, "Father Absence and Children's Cognitive Development," *Psychological Bulletin* 85, no. 2: 295–324.

139 **Some of the findings suggest:** M. Leidy, T. Schofield, and R. Parke, "Father's Contributions to Children's Social Development," in *Handbook of Father Involvement: Multidisciplinary Perspectives*, ed. N. J. Cabrera and C. S. Tamis-LeMonda (Oxford: Taylor and Francis, 2013).

139 **Other findings suggest no differences:** Goldstein, "Fathers' Absence and Cognitive Development of Children over a 3- to 5-Year Period."

139 **Some findings suggest benefits:** Mihaly Csikszentmihalyi, *Creativity: Flow and the Psychology of Discovery* (New York: Harper Perennial, 2009).

141 **My research and writings:** W. Damon, "Good? Bad? Or None of the Above? The Time-Honored Unavoidable Mandate to Teach Character," *Education Next* 5 (2): 20–28.

141 **I have written about the value of religious faith:** J. M. Mariano and W. Damon, "The Role of Spirituality and Religious Faith in Supporting Purpose in Adolescence," in *Positive Youth Development and Spirituality: From*

Theory to Research, ed. R. Lerner, R. Roeser, and E. Phelps (West Conshohocken, PA: Templeton Foundation Press, 2008), 210-230.

145 **One of my early papers:** For my early statement on this, see W. Damon, "Why Study Social-Cognitive Development?" *Human Development* 22: 206-212.

146 **The bottom line:** W. J. Lively and D. B. Bromley, *Person Perception in Childhood and Adolescence* (London: Wiley, 1973).

146 **The second dominant view:** L. Kohlberg, "The Study of Moral Development," in *Moral Development and Behavior*, ed. T. Lickona (New York: Holt, Rinehart, and Winston, 1976).

147 **While exploring children's social cognition:** W. Damon, *The Social World of the Child* (San Francisco: Jossey-Bass, 1977).

148 **I had made a bit of progress:** W. Damon, "The Development of Justice and Self-Interest during Childhood," in *The Justice Motive in Social Behavior*, ed. M. Lerner (New York: Plenum Press, 1981), 57-72; W. Damon and M. Killen, "Peer Interaction and the Process of Change in Children's Moral Reasoning," *Merrill-Palmer Quarterly* 28 (no. 3): 347-367.

149 **The initial result:** W. Damon and A. Colby, *The Power of Ideals: The Real Story of Moral Choice* (New York: Oxford University Press, 2015).

149 **The research that we published:** A. Colby and W. Damon, *Some Do Care: Contemporary Lives of Moral Commitment* (New York: The Free Press, 1992).

151 **Renamed "the Good Project":** See https://www.thegoodproject.org.

151 **Immediately after that:** I describe the core findings of this third, most recent phase of my research program in chapter 3 of this book.

152 **There has also been some important work:** B. Benard, *Fostering Resiliency in Kids: Protective Factors in Family, School, and Community* (Berkeley, CA: West Ed, 1991); Emmy E. Werner, *Through the Eyes of Innocents* (New York: Basic Books, 2001); K. Weir, "Maximizing Children's Resilience," in *Monitor on Psychology* (Washington, DC: American Psychological Association, 2017).

153 **"The uprising of 1968":** H. Gardner, *The Quest for Mind* (New York: Random House, 1972).

153 **"The moral reasoning":** E. L. Simpson, "Moral Development Research: A Case Study of Scientific Bias," *Human Development* 17: 81-106.

155 **In 1975, my old mentor:** R. Brown and R. Herrnstein, *Psychology* (Boston: Little, Brown, 1975).

156 **With an extremely talented and dedicated group:** W. Damon, ed.,
Handbook of Child Psychology: The Fifth Edition, 4 vols. (New York: John
Wiley and Sons, 1996); W. Damon and R. Lerner, eds., *Handbook of Child
Psychology: The Sixth Edition*, 4 vols. (New York: John Wiley and Sons, 2006).

156 **I revised the entire thing:** W. Damon, *The Moral Child: Nurturing Children's
Natural Moral Growth* (New York: The Free Press, 1990). Translated into
Italian, Japanese, German, Chinese, Polish, Korean, and Danish,
1995–2004.

156 **In the mid-1990s:** W. Damon, *Greater Expectations: Overcoming the Culture of
Indulgence in Our Homes and Schools* (New York: The Free Press, 1995).

157 **A follow-up book:** W. Damon, *The Youth Charter: How Communities Can
Work Together to Raise Standards for All Our Children* (New York: The Free
Press, 1997).

157 **At Stanford:** See the Stanford Center on Adolescence publications web
page: https://coa.stanford.edu/publications.

Chapter 7

165 **"The Great Game":** I use this term advisedly, not just because it is common in golf literature, but because it suggests the seriousness with which we
entranced golfers take the game. Another indication is a joke that I've
heard golfers pass around: "It's often said that golf imitates life, but actually
it's life that imitates golf." I refer to this golf "wisdom" here in order to
defend my use of my golfing experience as a worthwhile case in point of the
insights that flowed from my life review.

165 **In his bestselling 1972 book:** M. Murphy, *Golf in the Kingdom* (New York:
Viking, 1972).

165 **I've kept the scorecard:** I add this note with trepidation, hoping that it will
not mark me as a hopelessly befogged cultist. The ball I used that day was
one I had bought in my earlier pilgrimage to Updike's home course in
Massachusetts. At St. Andrews, I played far better than my usual game,
scoring an 85 from the back tees and parring the famous Road Hole (all
attested to on a scorecard signed by my Scottish caddy). The really amazing
thing was that, over the course's eighteen treacherous holes, I never lost the
ball. It now sits in my basket without a single noticeable mark, as if it were
brand-new. Does that sound slightly mystical, or what?

Chapter 8

180 **Research by Robert Emmons:** R. Emmons, *Thanks! How the New Science of Gratitude Can Make You Happier* (New York: Hachette Book Group, 2007).

181 **In writings on "civic virtue":** H. Malin, P. Ballard, and W. Damon, "Civic Purpose: An Integrated Construct for Understanding Civic Development in Adolescence," *Human Development* 58:103–130.

182 **"If we will be quiet and ready enough":** S. J. Cramer, ed., *I to Myself: An Annotated Selection from the Journal of Henry D. Thoreau* (New Haven, CT: Yale University Press, 2007).

186 **For an older person:** For one of the finest treatments of aging gracefully, see M. Freedman, *How to Live Forever: The Enduring Power of Connecting the Generations* (New York: Hachette Book Group, 2018).

186 **I acquired more energy:** Marc Freedman calls this familiar type of aging "the Golden Years myth." I once heard a delightful talk from Pastor Rick Warren in which he mentioned resisting the idea of retiring to "a sunny beach to have drinks with little umbrellas in them." This image always makes me smile whenever I think about ways of spending my time when I reach my post-employment years.

189 **"the art and science of reminiscing":** Barbara Haight and Jeffery Webster, *The Art and Science of Reminiscing: Theory, Research, Methods, and Applications* (Washington, DC: Taylor and Francis, 1995).

192 **"prospective thinking":** Martin E. P. Seligman, Peter Railton, Roy F. Baumeister, and Chandra Sripada, *Homo Prospectus* (New York: Oxford University Press, 2017).

192 **This idea is compatible:** See, for example, C. Peterson and M. Seligman, *Character Strengths and Virtues: A Handbook and Classification* (New York: Oxford University Press, 2004).